A Journey Into the Light

Volume Two

PENSATIA

The Euclid Publishing Company
New York, N. Y.

THE PUBLISHED WORK OF PENSATIA
(Helen Merrick Bond)

Contents

Living Words From the Master

DEDICATED TO FRANK

With Love

Prelude

AGAIN, the Master H spoke within my heart:
"Write, Pensatia, my living words to man. Come when and where you will, my words will reach you. Journey with me and record."

Silence prevailed.

I arose from that inner communion knowing, with God's help, my pen will relay as I receive.

PENSATIA

✿ Chapter One

I
T WAS a bright sunny day. Soft, clear air prevailed over the river waters when came he, the Master, speaking: "Hear now my words. May they sink deep within the reader's consciousness.

"Life today, in these years of the '70's, proclaims a new star has risen, yet man sees it not. It is the Star of the Magi shining again out to man. It is the star telling of the Aquarian Dawn. Look up! Behold it! It shows the way to the Most High Mountain. It is the Star of Hope for man's liberation from his self-made chains.

"Here in quiet glen or beside river waters, while walking in green valleys or in the majestic silence of night's hush, when day breaks through the rising sun, I am your heart's temple. In the Cathedral of the Soul I come revealing my living words. Record them, that man may know my love.

"Listen now to the answers to questions often asked by the uninitiated.

Question one: "Why are some men weak and others strong?"

Answer: "Pensatia, man weaves his strength or weakness from past lives. He has created his weakness. Only he can redeem weakness through strength. Only man can sever chains he has forged in other incarnations. All alcoholism, prostitution and dope addiction were first sired with man's consent. Any time, with God and the Masters' aid, man can transmute negative karma into positive. Such is the Creator's law of mercy. Every man can build anew, and ever God gives to the prodigal son the fatted calf."

Question Two: "Why are the strong attracted to the weak, and vice versa?"

Answer: "One is always drawn to those needing moral support. Even so, the strong gravitate to weakness to test

7

their inner fiber. Each can help the other if willing to learn. Often, such loves are mated and lo, a miracle comes forth, for love conquers all. Yet each must be true to that 'Something above them' — God, the Masters and nature. To achieve heavenly or spiritual consciousness, man must dare greatly. One must be still, listen, and obey."

Question Three: "Are initiations important? Cannot one attain Cosmic Consciousness without them?"

Answer: "No, never can one attain the Living Rose objectively or in slumber without initiation or an awareness of a new field of realization. Otherwise, the student is forever outside the pale of Cosmic altitude. One must meet and face his esoteric initiations, which come to all when ripe upon the Path. Only through initiation will the chakras open and vibrate rightly. Study, read all esoteric books, talk with cosmic minded men. Yet without personal initiation, all leads to naught. Initiation is awakening of one's inner self. It must be sired by the Flame of Isis. It springs from the fire of the crucibles. Man knows when he has been initiated. From that moment, he speaks with authority. Initiation is one's esoteric diploma, the password to the Most High Mountain."

Question Four: "Does the esoteric Path guarantee health and life everlasting?"

Answer: "This is a deep and honest question, and deserves an honest answer. In Cosmic terms, I would say, yes, granted that the exact formula is obeyed; otherwise, until all ingredients are attained by the disciple, the lack of just *one* will bar him from what he seeks.

"Life, not death, is ever God's gift to man. The secret of the ages is written back of the sun. When man is ready for the answer, it will be 'Yes.' Seek and you will find. Ask and it will be given to you. Man already has that for which he seeks. Be aware. Life is in death, and death is in life. Only by the Alchemical Marriage can the two live eternally. This is one of the deeper mysteries. Persevere and you will know."

Question Five: "How may one know when he meets his true affinity?"

Answer: "This, too, is a deep question. Listen and heed my words. One's affinity comes when one is ripe for such — early or late in life. Each, or both, may be married legally. Yet heed this and know: When *true* affinities meet, the Lords of Karma bring it to pass. All barriers are dissolved, not by man, but by Cosmic law. It is a feeling of togetherness, a fulfillment of mind, heart, body and soul; a transcendent experience, never to be forgotten. It is a knowing of belonging, one to the other. Age, passion, materialism, have no part in it. Affinities are sired from lives far past. The meeting and the earthly mating are inevitable. The fulfillment must be. Already wed inwardly, the outer rites must follow. This is not attained by hurting another. As above so below, as below so above. Ever give gratitude to God and the Masters when Love so shines upon you. Embrace it, else it will depart for many incarnations."

Question Six: "Is regeneration a fact or a myth?"

Answer: "Regeneration is a Cosmic fact, yet it only comes about through initiation and spiritual awakening. Walking the Path of the Rose and Lotus, or the Way of the Christus, is the only way to regeneration of body, mind and heart. Attaining the Golden Dawn brings forth regeneration on all points of the triangle. This comes slowly, or can come with suddenness. Persevere, students, neophytes, disciples, and regeneration will be yours."

Question Seven: "When an illness is diagnosed as terminal, can it be cured by Cosmic healing?"

Answer: "Yes, absolutely. Let those so suffering empty themselves of negation; let forgiveness fill the heart and only Faith and Love be. Then in gratitude, ask: 'If it be the Father's Will, let healing be.' Then arise in consciousness and *know* you are healed. Keep this up. No matter the outward appearances, *know inwardly it is so*. The outer must follow. According to your faith, it will be. This is the infallible law. When doctors give up, God takes over. Give gratitude."

Question Eight: "How about negative karma? How does one liquidate it?"

Answer: "By about-face, forgiving yourself and others and henceforth creating good karma, giving your heart to God and Jesus Christ. By erasing all negation from the subconscious and ever seeking the Holy Grail and the Rose of Life. Love all, forgive all, and walk the Path. Thus will your wrong karma be liquidated."

Question Nine: "Are the Masters' words infallible?"

Answer: "When taken from Akasha. When the Hierarchical Masters speak out through the heart, or to their disciples, know what is spoken will be — yet in God's time and place, not man's. Trust the Masters, God and the Christus. It is the Father's Will to give you the kingdom."

"Now, Pensatia, let's cease questioning and talk of meditation and communion with nature and man. When one is schooled in the foundation of meditation, one realizes it is only a beautiful silent relationship with God, the Masters, with nature and humanity. One realizes he is a living temple where any time, anywhere, he may be still and hear, sense and feel the still, small voice of the soul. One may or may not attend the outer churches, for his real cathedral is within the heart and soul. Henceforth, in simplicity and trust, one's life becomes a living prayer of service and homage to the Creator. Often such persons are denounced by the ignorant masses as atheists, when the truth is they are closer to God than those who judge. So beware of such judgment as you journey through life. Remember, every sincere meditation brings one closer to the profound simplicity of the inner wisdom of the heart. Ask, and you will receive. Seek, and you will find. Persevere and give not up in the dark night of growth. Know that you have not been forsaken by the Father or the venerable Masters.

"Arise with the song of the woods and streams, the voice of the high mountains and the music of the spheres pouring out the hum of creation. Reach up beyond the outer sordidness and chaos to the simple, everyday joys of true friendship and the pure love of hearts mated. Enjoy immortal art, great books, the happiness and mirth in nature and man. These are the cornerstones of illumination. Never forget — before one attains the Rose of Life, let one become a good human first. Let one be strong and steadfast in the homely virtues of honesty, love and outgoing oneness with all life. Ever seek the kernel within the nut of life. Ever have something green and growing within the home. Let your room reflect the harmony of God and nature, that those who pass your way will find peace and comfort within."

As I, Pensatia, listened to the strong, yet gentle voice of the Master H, precious incense from transcendent dimensions enveloped my consciousness. It was a happy, natural attunement within the temple of my heart. I was grateful to have this sacred privilege of recording these journeys with the Master H, our elder Brother who has trod the Way and won. May we ever seek to do likewise.

I look out my window, watching the swift-moving traffic on the by-pass, and below, the river winding out to the sea. As I gaze upon the tall eucalyptus trees and the summer riot

11

of color, and listen to the song of nesting birds, I sense God and the Master's love breathing through each and all. Now again, the Master speaks.

"Pensatia, man and nature must walk and work together, reflecting the bounty of the Creator. There must be no demarcation between nature and man and God. At one, they must and will reflect the Aquarian Age.

"It is through imbibing the cosmic influx of the seasons that we become more aware of our divine heritage. One should, when possible, partake of the seasons' visitation. There is a cleansing inner baptism in the flow of the rain, even as the thirsty earth partakes and renews itself. So man is renewed by contact with nature. It is through the stillness of the heart center that the inner wisdom of the Rose and Lotus is made known to man. Until man can speak a common tongue with woods, fields and streams; until one feels and senses the silent love of plant and flower; until one is at home away from the city hustle and lights, and finds peace in the chirp of a cricket and song of a bird, and is truly a brother to the 'wild,' one cannot progress far on the Path. A man of true meditation is at one with all nature and gives God reverence for His mighty works.

"Yes, Pensatia, meditation is simply walking with God and hearing Him within the silence of the heart. It is oneness with the Father, and trust and faith as one travels step by step to one's divine soul awakening. All Cosmic books repeat over and over the esoteric wisdom of the ages. Yes, Pensatia, man and nature together must reflect the Creator.

"Man is slowly and surely evolving into the superior man of cosmic consciousness. The seed of America's tomorrow must and will spring from its divine inception of the Declaration of Independence, and its allegiance to God. The open mind of a Lincoln, Paine, Jefferson, Webster — all the immortals of history — and the impact of the common man, place their indelible stamp upon the coming age of our to-morrows. The fermenting chaos of the present will be trans-muted into the fertility and peace of the Aquarian Brother-hood. So, with patience and faith, live through these trying times, ever shining out to life. Love from the heart's temple; forgive. Speak only words of comfort, of quickening alle-giance to infallible Cosmic law. Ever let the Aquarian Waterpitcher sprinkle its purifying waters upon you. Thus will you be prepared for the esoteric renaissance of the Brotherhood of Man and the Golden Dawn. Let no word of negation speak from your lips, lest you hasten self-destruction. Cultivate music which uplifts heart and soul. Meditate at hush of evening hour in woods, beside nature's waters, or in the quiet of thyself anywhere. There the still small voice will speak to you; you will attune with the in-finite; a new life will be yours. Seek the Holy Grail, the living Rose and Lotus. Capture the wide-spreading hum of wings of the gray geese as they fly through air and over waters. Lift thy nostrils to the tang of ocean splendor and craggy mountains, to the brave trees which live through storm and vicissitudes of raw nature. Learn to speak with all animals.

"Yes, Pensatia, and you who read, lift up your eyes to God and His manifold creation. Worship at the shrine of the Essene Christ. Light the candle of the Rose in thy heart and bear the light out to the wide, wide world. Thus will one triumph and ever transmute the lesser into the higher, and leaven all into one. Let laughter and joy kindle the same in all who pass your way. Thus will you be truly serving God and the Masters."

❀ Chapter Two

IN THE quiet of my heart's temple, the Master spoke again.

"Pensatia, listen well and record."

Hearing his clear, graphic words, I obeyed.

"I would transport you to the Cosmic design of all creation."

I donned my travelling cape of white, and partook of the green pellet of balance. Thus we journeyed swiftly as light beyond all planets to that golden Temple of the Sun. Here, seated around a circular table, were the Lords of Karma, the venerable judges of karmic justice. From afar, high above, the All-Seeing Eye looked down.

Before these men of God was a great and mighty book. A gong sounded out. A name was called, and the Lords of Karma spoke.

"All mankind have their names, deeds, thoughts, big and little, etched upon the akashic print. All is reviewed at certain intervals. The sowing of man's acts are reaped in green harvest, or lessons to be learned over.

"When certain karma is liquidated, the chimes sound out the Cosmic Gong, and a desire comes true; a dream is fulfilled; healing comes; a prayer is answered. Here, only justice prevails. Cause and effect claims and receives its just dues. All sudden legacies — love realized after long years, healing after much suffering — all happen by redeemed negative karma, or the harvest of happy karma.

"This reading of the Karmic Log goes on eternally by the custodians of the karmic records of all humanity. So you see, Pensatia, nothing happens by chance. By man's repentance and about-face, by giving allegiance to God and the Christus, by facing one's mistakes, man liquidates negative karma and learns to create only happy karmic blessings.

"Those who live by self-pride and ego will reap the de-

14

structive effect of what they sow. All must be transmuted into Light, Life and Love. The blessings of good karma often seem like a miracle, or to result from the waving of a magic wand. Yet all is according to justice and order. If a man would only realize every act and thought has a cause and effect, and that to reap green harvest, one must generate the seeds of positive action. A sweeping away of all dross must take place. All resentments and non-forgiveness must be replaced by love, joy, peace and humor. Thus will your karma be free of sorrow and lack. Thus will you walk in the wisdom of God and the Master. Thus will you find the Kingdom of Heaven within and sip from the Holy Grail.

"Pensatia, here in the Temple of Light beyond the earthly sun, you behold the law and order of the Creator's justice for man. Ever know, man destroys — not God! As one walks the Path and obeys the karmic law, he becomes regenerated, radiant in the Golden Dawn. The heart sings in the unity of all. Karma no longer holds one back. Man speaks a common tongue with the ancients and the sages of today, and walks Earth and Heaven as one. The long dark night of the soul is justified. One walks henceforth in the Golden Dawn, a man dedicated in the Cosmic Light of the Most High Mountain. Such is the fiat of the Creator: Man serving in the splendor of his divine birthright.

"When man reaches this state of consciousness, he is fully prepared to live in the Aquarian Age. Its Cosmic climate is his by right of attainment. He has weathered the crucibles and alchemy of life, and now is able to make gold and give gold. Truly, the Stone and Elixir are his to use for the service of mankind. The Jewel in the Lotus has appeared. The Living Rose blooms. Love regenerates all things.

"Pensatia, behold the Love rays from the Golden Dawn."

15

Gazing upward, I felt the pink dew of the Rose of Life spiralling through me, felt the healing bath of the fountain of the Waters of Life. I was handed a silver talisman, with the All-Seeing Eye engraved within a triangle.

"Keep this in your consciousness. It levels all illness into harmony and divine order. One who attains this has the key to earthly and heavenly riches. It liquidates the dregs of past negative karma, and infuses the Sun rays through one's body. Even as this Cosmic talisman is yours, so will you be attracted to its earthly duplicate."

I gave thanks to the Creator, God of all, and to the Masters, and asked, "How long before the earthly realization will be?"

He, the Master H, smiled, saying:

"Be aware. As thy faith, so be it. Many wait long for their harvest when it is before them. Accept what is given you. It is your gift from the Cosmic Father. Have faith. No matter how dark the night, dawn will come. All of a sudden, healing, material supply or love long denied will be. Yes, the Creator will not give you a stone when you ask for bread.

"So, ever arise, O reader, with joy perform your daily tasks. Yet, with high vision, bear on to the High Mountain.

"Now, Pensatia, let's discuss what a realist is.

"So many who hold to the orthodox view pride themselves as being such. They are so far away from the real facts, they only expose their ignorance. One can only love and have compassion. Only light your lamp and exemplify the esoteric Path. Know, only knowledge of the whole of life is real — the spiritual, mental and physical. Until man is aware of the three points of the Triangle, he is not, and never can be, a realist. Those who think thusly will have a sad awakening. Yes, ever is it so, the so-called realists deny their spiritual heritage. As above, below; as below, above.

16

They work not from the finished kingdom, but only from the letter, not the spirit. Such persons live life after life stagnating in their rock-bound ignorance, until, in time, they become petrified. Now, in this Aquarian Age, such men cannot survive into the full glory of the Golden Dawn. Self-deceived, always having excuses, they scoff at anything they don't understand, or care to. Many are lovable, so-called good people without imagination or humor. Seek not to change them. The Law of Karma will see to that.

"No one can come into esoteric wisdom or know the Hierarchal Masters until they shed the human ego and, as a little child, let go all dogma, orthodoxy and intolerance. One must have an open mind, an open heart, and want God more than life. Only then will the Master draw nearer. Remember, a realist is never negative, never rock-bound, but always fluid and open to Cosmic impact. A realist is never set, but is ever learning, expanding in awareness and walking the Path to the Most High Mountain within one's heart. No one but himself (or an earth-shaking experience) may awaken one out of his set dogmatic graveyard.

"As one builds wrongly, so must one dissolve and build anew. Yet, of those who read my recorded books from Pensatia, not all will respond. Sad to say, some will close the books, saying in their conceit, 'I am a realist. This is only fiction!' Such is the curse of the unawakened. Yet ever remember — because one has evolved to a higher state of consciousness, and has truly earned it, he should not be puffed up. Remember that once in some life you, too, were rock-bound and set. By example — love, meet these people on their own plane. Seek the common denominator in all things. Fashion yourself after old Mother Nature. In her Earth Garden, weeds and roses grow side by side. All shades of color mingle and are one. Everything is variegated. Yes, learn from nature. If one does not love nature or man, he cannot love God, for all nature, all humanity is of God.

"Now, Pensatia, depart and walk earthward. Reflect and ponder well on my words, ever conceived in the Finished Kingdom, and so it will be earthly. That is the law.

"Know also, often, or otherwise, whenever or wherever you put your pen to this recording, so will I be with you."

❀ Chapter Three

THE MASTER H, he, the friend, the Counselor of Man, spoke again in the silence of my heart. As I listen, so do I record his living words to man.

"Pensatia, what one lacks, one must, in some incarnation, acquire. The lack is shown in one's birth chart. If one would study real astrology, he soon would discover and learn where he has failed. There are lessons that he yet must learn. To know astrology is to know thyself. It takes courage to face up to the past and to build anew. Yet, it must be done. Only when one faces his mundane astrological chart is he ready for esoteric astrology and the way to the Masters. Yes, ever the Creator gives man the blueprint he himself has written in ages past, up to and including the present.

"Man must liquidate past mistakes. Again and again and again he must analyze his progress, outwardly and inwardly. As a realist, one must face up to lessons yet to be learned. Man must know what he has earned and that which he yet has to earn. The birth chart and Tarot readings and the Book of Thoth will supply this knowledge. Through meditation and obedience to the Path, man will find the truth of the Masters. Always, truth is within, without. One must

18

see, feel and know the within of nature, man and life before he knows the mundane. This is the law of the Creator; the simple and profound are both one. The last pangs of the Piscean Age are being transmuted into the Golden Dawn of the Aquarian Age.

"The transits of the major planets through Libra and Sagittarius will relay their Cosmic impact. Thus do nations and man have the opportunity to evolve into their Cosmic heritage.

"Alchemy, divine and mundane, brings forth the true Stone and Elixir. This can never be a spurious undertaking, but a dedicated work in the crucibles. Dare, do and be silent and gold will be.

"To know himself, man must first have a great desire, then honestly face all past negative karma. He must seek entrance to the outer portal leading him to the esoteric school of the true Golden Dawn.

"Go forth, O reader; search and you will find that life on earth is a glorious privilege. To attain one's place in soul evolution and earth service, rest assured there are no short cuts — no quick magic of results. Each earns, through initiation, all the green harvest and the knowing of the Masters. Man is the alchemist; he alone can bring forth oneness with the Father, with all nature and humanity. No drugs, no LSD, can do aught but destroy. Remember, and steer clear of such. Walk day by day in faith and trust. Seek the esoteric Path of the Essene, Jesus, and follow through to the Golden Dawn. Thus will strength and wisdom be yours. Where others doubt, you will know.

"Seek the words of those who have left their imprint through pen, music, art, and the living example of the Rose of Life. Go to nature, meditate in the greenery of woods, streams and hills, or on the vast oceans and high mountains, or in the peace and quiet of your home. Communicate with all who pass your way. Thus will new doors open, circulation of Cosmic breezes awaken and stir you to action. Let the waters of life pour over and through you. All that needs cleansing comes forth in the Dew of the Rose.

"Pensatia," the Master continued, "the Bridge of Vision is open to all men who prepare and dare to cross it. One is only half a man who seeks not the Golden Dawn. To know only the objective mundane is a fool's quest. A man is only as big as his soul consciousness and his love out to life. Only an open heart and mind leads man to wisdom. Those who have not these credentials are living zombies, already stagnating in their narrow dogma and closed chakras.

"As the rivers ever flow out to the vast oceans, so man within himself must ever flow and seek the Most High Mountain of the Living Rose. There is within man himself all the wisdom of the ages and the infinite design for his progress. Yet man must mine it through the crucibles and bring forth pure gold. This is the ordained work of all mankind — the birth of the Philosopher's Stone and Elixir.

"The sooner one starts, the sooner one reaps the green harvest of the illumined heart. Yet know, Pensatia, one must start in the loam of earth discipline. In the low karmic altitude of past and present cause and effect, one must dedicate heart and mind to the finding of the Golden Dawn. There can be no short cuts or spurious experimentation. All endeavors must be according to Cosmic formula. Exact is the way of the Path, exact the way to the Most High Mountain. Yet, most glorious the victory."

Sitting under the spiritual aura of the Master, a higher octave of consciousness was experienced by me.

"Know, Pensatia," said the Venerable One, "all wisdom spoken from within must stand the censorship of God, the

Creator, and your earthly reason. There must be harmony and oneness between the two. In reality, all rapport is sired from the Christus and the Temple of the Soul.

"Nature and one's heart are the open door to the Masters and the friends of man. It is as natural as breathing to seek and find the Master within. Sincerity, dedication to the Christus, joy in service and love will inevitably draw one through the open door of the esoteric Path. To seek the astral phenomena and occult power will close the entrance to the true Way of the Living Rose. Remember, and seek not 'fool's gold,' but the alchemical Stone and the Elixir.

"Let me explain that infinite law now," H said. " 'As above so below, as below so above.' It contains a great latitude of understanding, infallible, yet relative to each student of the Way. To understand and be inwardly initiated into the sacred Archives means wisdom and balance to all esoteric students.

"In the Above, in the great Akasha, are all records of man's pilgrimage through Earth experience. Also, all nature, from weeds to roses, from the primeval to the now. In the immortal weave of Akasha is pictured the Golden Age of Aquarius. The unevolved student and the ignorant masses tune in to the negative aspect of this cosmic law, thus reaping the cause and effect of their actions, while those disciples of Rose and Lotus, of the Essene, Jesus, the Christed One, use the positive Cosmic aspect of the law. Remember, both are above, as both are below. In earthly parlance, one may seek and find the highest octave of living and service. He may aspire to be the true alchemist, learning the sure way through the crucibles and initiation, or seek the spurious allure of the negation of phenomena and occult powers for self. Whatever man chooses, so does the Above reflect the Below, and the Below, the Above. As one seeks

21

the spiritual aboveness of the law, he then gravitates to the spiritual aboveness below, and thus transmutes the earthly aspect to the heavenly, and aids at the same time in transporting the heavenly into the earthly. To know and understand this law is the fulfillment of man's attainment. Without this awareness, no one can be integrated into the oneness of all life.

"As above, below; as below, above — which means: that which you seek below, you will also find above; that which you seek above, you will find below. To balance and integrate and fuse the both into the Cosmic whole is the work of mankind. The dross must be eliminated out of earthly loam and infused with the Above, and the Above must wed the Earth nature and become one. It is a gradual process to achieve this initiation into the esoteric law. Yet, early or late, one must awaken to this fact: As above so below, as below so above. This one law embraces the Living Word and secret of God's design for man. Know this law and you will achieve true illumination. This is what the Aquarian Age will teach mankind — the universal oneness of humanity.

"In the Golden Dawn, man will come forth the divine alchemist. Woman will become the earthly mate of man. Each will have experienced the Alchemical Marriage and be worthy to know the unification of earthly and heavenly love. All nature will respond to the Cosmic awakened man.

"So, with courage and faith, bear on through the chaos of this dying century. Prepare for the Golden Dawn of a new tomorrow. Learn the lessons of today.

"People and nations, transmute negative karma into Light, Life and Love."

 Chapter Four

THE MASTER came in the full bloom of a Caribbean summer day. Happy frolicking breezes played among the poinciana and the bougainvillea. The yellow and white frangipani drank in God's sun.

Came he, the friend of man, walking softly by the river bank. My inner consciousness felt and knew the rapport, that close bond of student and Guru.

"Pensatia, reflect on nature and learn thereof. Learn from trees, and flowers, from the winds and the sea. Harsh are the storms of life. They lash, aye, kill — yet only that man build anew.

"When man lives in love and harmony with nature, then indeed will all life exemplify true brotherhood. Love, that immortal flow of the Word, will ignite the Golden Dawn within man himself. The Edenic Garden will then come forth for man in full effulgence of consciousness. Man will be at home in all dimensions of the above and below.

"O glorious is the way to our lost Shangri-la! Strong the discipline, yet most enlightening the result. Out of the blackness of ignorance, man arises in the majesty of the living Rose of Life. The man becomes Christed, the Christed becomes human.

"All Cosmic esoteric books repeat over and over the Way of Illumination. This cannot be bought or attained through another's realization. Each must travel the Path within and bring forth the white Stone and Elixir. No short cuts will aid you to fulfillment. Rather, they will hinder and destroy, for only that earned can give birth to the Holy Babe within the manger of one's heart.

"Yes, Pensatia, it is an exacting road. Yet many vistas of green oases and communion with the Master compensate for the steep climb to the Most High Mountain. Attar of

23

Roses and the sweet mystery of life are revealed step by step. Yes, every ascent upward partakes of the Song of the Spheres. The Golden Dawn shines through the dark night of the soul, ever guiding one onward. One will glimpse the goal, shining bright from yon High Mountain. The Masters stand ever in the background, watching and aiding, according to the Law of Karma. Step by step the neophyte, the postulant, and then the disciple, become aware that only decadence and betrayal (personally and nationally) of the Cosmic law can carry man and nations into oblivion and death. All must make the decision to become oriented to their divine design, or to follow the way of all flesh. Neither God nor the Masters can make it for you.

"The Word went forth — the Creator's plan for man. Yet, man must seek and find the esoteric gate and climb to the Temple of the Sun within one's heart. Only thusly can one survive the Golden Age of Aquarius. No longer can man cut his lifeline of oneness with nature and the Masters and live. As above so below, as below so above. Ponder deeply on these immortal laws.

"Now, Pensatia, we will discuss healing. Know this one infallible law: Nothing is impossible with God!

"In extreme cases, when healing seems beyond the doctors' aid, know and act in Faith. God will hear and answer. Healing must come if karma permits. Even then, in the twinkling of an eye, that, too, can be liquidated and health be restored. Mind, body and soul must work as one. Love must flow like the sun out to life. In every aspect of life, material or otherwise, the law is the same: 'Ask, and you will receive. Seek, and you will find. Love, and you will receive love.' Have faith. Look ever to the Star of Hope. With these credentials you cannot fail.

"Do not discard a dedicated doctor. God works through

24

many channels. Have faith, even when all seems for naught, and if initiated into the Golden Flame, stay in it. All illness is finally transmuted in its Love Rays. Yet enter not until ready and guided by the Guru. Slow and steady obedience to the boot training is essential in all authentic esoteric orders.

"Now let us discuss love and sex. Know, love is not sex, and sex is not love. Love is sired from soul alchemy. Sex is the earthly communion of true love. Without the soul rapport, it is lust, and destroys. All who betray its sacred meaning can never attain the High Mountain until they seek and find the Alchemical Marriage. Such is the Cosmic mandate from the Creator. Love is, indeed, a many splendored thing, when mated under the stars of heaven. Only then can man and woman be really wed. All other unions are only legal ties. So beware of infatuation, which is of the physical senses only. Ever seek that triune union of heart, mind and soul. Such marriages last beyond the earthly sphere. Prepare to be worthy of such, else it pass you by and you know it not. When such a meeting occurs, know it is not coincidental. Like a tidal wave, it will sweep away all barriers — in God's way, not man's. One will know for a surety when one meets thusly. The eyes will lock and a great peace will flow, one to the other. You will know. Even though you may be parted for a while, your destiny will bring you together. So love like the sun, universally, with pureness of heart. Keep your love high like a star in the sky. It may be early or late in life, but meet one will when the Lords of Karma sound the Cosmic gong. When this occurs, hesitate not to commune, each with the other. Thus will health and fulfillment be yours. Without love, one shrivels and dies. So love abundantly, even without return, and know your own will come to you. Read 'The Prophet,' by

25

Gibran. Therein is the secret of love. Yes, love is the key to life everlasting. Remember — and love.

"Now, Pensatia, let us go and resume our talks in the cool of the Cosmic Garden. Partake of the green pellet and follow me."

I obeyed. In conscious rapport we traveled in our Body of Light to the high ramparts and shady trees and green of the Garden of Light. The song of birds of beautiful colored plumage greeted us. The silver waters of life flowed by, vibrant, yet peaceful. There on the banks of that infinite river esoteric, we sat on the Cosmic loam. There was an amber softness in the atmosphere. The variegated flowers grew spontaneously like sparkling jewels. Throughout the Garden the fragrance was as the lotus and attar of roses. A warm closeness threaded its rapport down to earth vibrations.

"As above so below, as below so above," spoke H. "Yet how few live in conscious awareness of the infallible law. Thus the masses cannot participate in the wonder and transcendent beauty of this majestic Garden. Yet always it waits through the years for man to awake and search for the gate to this esoteric meeting place."

Relaxed, we sat on the emerald bank in the shade of large outspreading trees, and in silence absorbed the exhilarating splendor of the Garden. I was conscious of men and women walking together in beautiful affection, as though their oneness was of heart and soul. Love seemed to flow from them in golden streams. One felt uplifted and happy as they passed by. In the distance sloping hills and charming homes adorned the panoramic scenery.

"What means this?" I asked the Master.

"Here is the earned harvest of those who, in transition, are united with their true affinity. Here they reap their

26

home, love and expression in Cosmic vibration. All the beauty and glory of life are held in escrow for man to reap when he has earned such. Even though karma often denies such on earth, know in death one finds fulfillment and the love man was meant to have. Thus, in earth life, only his self-made cause and effect bars the realization of that which he seeks. Hold to the Star of Hope, knowing God ever seeks to give you the pure desires of your heart. Be not dismayed at disappointments or partings, or that all seems naught. Look not back, but ever forward. Dare greatly. Live out to life with joy and faith. Remember, God, the Creator, knows all that has your signature on it will come to you. As one evolves and attains self-conscious opening of the chakras, one may transport his consciousness any time to higher dimensions of awareness. This is true of all disciples and initiates.

"In this Garden, sadness and friction do not exist. This is the Garden of tranquility and love. Here one walks in splendor and infinite beauty. Here the Masters walk and talk with their students. At intervals, here by the banks of the river of silver waters, we answer questions from the students. Here the rays from the Most High Mountain make pure and life-giving the air.

"Remember, all life is a state of consciousness, an awareness of the higher dimensions. Man must learn the 'way back home,' and walk and commune with the Masters. Thus only will peace come and the Brotherhood of Man be realized. One must have faith when the tide is out, and *know* all will be. Only as one follows the Path all the way will one be able to reach and walk in this esoteric Cosmic Garden.

✽ Chapter Five

I, PENSATIA, felt weary and at low ebb, as though the tide would never come in. A lassitude was heavy within my heart. The Master's presence seemed far away. A cold desolation crept over me like a poisonous reptile.

"Yes," came the strong, gentle voice of the Master, standing once more at my side. A great light poured over and through me.

"O ye of little faith!" spoke he. "Know you not, Pensatia, even unto the Masters come these moments of utter despair, as though all is futile, as though the Golden Dawn is not? Yet arise, one must, and know the Star of Hope ever guides one through such moments. Know the Master ever *is* and stands by."

His words vibrated through all my being, as a lamp shining in the darkness. Yes, with pen, I now felt inspired anew to record these Living Words from the Master.

"Pensatia, remember, when these dark moments come, they are in reality our friendly teachers; they are the challenges to our faith. Without these black ebbs, we would never realize our progress — our fitness to go on. If we lift our faith ever to the Star of Hope, this despair will pass and we will arise with new strength and courage. Even when one has arrived and is stabilized in the Golden Flame, yet as long as one is in Earth incarnation, again and again will one have moments of lack and futility. If, at these times, one seeks to escape the testing in drink or drugs, one only destroys his esoteric progress and, if continued, pays dearly in karmic cause and effect. This is more so if one is on the Path. To know and not obey is against Cosmic law. When once man enters the self-conscious Path of the Masters, he cannot digress without paying a high penalty, perhaps for several incarnations. Yes, Pensatia, the Path demands the

28

utmost dedication. Yet this is never forced. Man ever has free will. Readers, remember and know.

"Pensatia, look about you in this Cosmic altitude of Garden. Above all, do you not sense the harmony between man and nature? Is there not a current of golden love bonding bird, beast, flower and shrub with the human heart? Yes, here is the divine pattern for Earth. As above so below, as below so above.

"There is a place not yet discovered which truly reflects this esoteric law. Only when man himself exemplifies this mandate will the Earth Shangri-la come. Man himself must pioneer and discover the lost glory. Man must awake and seek the hidden door within the heart. This Garden is accessible to all who attain the initiations of the Rose and Lotus. Peace profound, the music of the spheres, the communion with all life, the glory of crossing the Bridge of Vision, the love transcendent will be his. All this will be, as the faithful disciple learns and applies the divine formula. To attain the altitude and peace of this esoteric Garden is to have communion with both Earth and the ramparts of Cosmic dimensions. This is, indeed, the Shangri-la of the soul, the blessed rapport with the Masters and the high strata of consciousness. Here, one reaps the green harvest of his toil and labor in the crucibles. One is at ease, as it were, in Cosmic dimensions. He lives and breathes the effulgence of the Waters of Life. One knows so far every step of the Way. He is ready to travel on. But one may ever rest and renew one's self here in this beautiful Garden of Life, in its Cosmic splendor. To reach this Elysian Garden is indeed the golden gift of the Creator to all who seek the Most High Mountain of the illumined heart. So does the Creator bless all who walk the way of the Rose and the Lotus."

Now the Master H did take me to that vast chamber where the essence of all herbs and plant life, discovered and yet to be discovered, are to be found. The healing essence and vibrational rays are caught and segregated in the Department of Cosmic Remedies for all diagnosis. Here the Guardian stands ready to diagnose and dispense those remedies for the disciples' physical needs. Only those who have attained the Golden Dawn are prepared to sip from this alchemical reservoir of healing essences.

The venerable Guardian showed us a black drink, saying, "This is the cleansing liquid which purifies the arteries and makes them pliable. To take this three times a day cures hardening of the arteries. One should also use a green pellet. This equalizes the blood pressure and renews the circulation. When all else fails, take the green pellet. These healing essences are all of Cosmic vibrations. Try them not unless directed by the Master and you are initiated in the Golden Dawn. When ready, you will know. Meanwhile, use the earthly remedies.

"Remember, in the Golden Flame is contained all the essence of earthly and heavenly attributes. If one would have a healthy complexion, leave off cosmetics. Use a good soap and water and blend in a Cosmic tincture of Rose Dew."

The pink vial of this rose liquid which he handed us had a purple stopper.

"Take a sip of this any time, anywhere, as often as you desire. Also rub it over the face. In time one will have the complexion of youth."

He now showed us a fiery red plant extract, saying, "This is the essence for the hair. Rub this in the scalp every day. Soon the hair will be healthy and, where thin, it will grow. These medicinal Cosmic drinks are the blessings and rewards of the Path. Enter the Mystic Way and travel to the Most High Mountain. Doctors and biochemists are daily discovering the earthly signature of such. Some day, in the full Aquarian Age, the duplicates will be discovered on Earth."

Now the Cosmic Pharmacist brought forth what appeared to be an onion.

"This is the divine essence of the onion," he said. "Squeeze the juice on the eyes and all cataracts and glaucoma will be healed. Do this at night before sleep. It can be used any time, anywhere. In Pensatia's other books, I have mentioned the red berry and the orange. These, taken every day, will heal the spleen and prevent anemia. Also, the green leaf with silver streaks brings elimination and is a tonic to the stomach."

It was most interesting to sense and listen and partake of these drinks.

Now spoke the Master H.

"Pensatia, partake. Thus will you be fortified to record my messages. Stand in the spiral bath of the living Waters of Life every day. Thus will one be regenerated and live long in service to God and the Masters. . . .

"Now, Pensatia, what questions would you like to ask?"

Amber dusk was settling over the Cosmic Garden. A hush, a peace prevailed. It was as though God, the Creator, was there, as though man was at one with all life. I felt completely renewed. Anticipating the answers from the Master, I asked,

Question: "When can one expect fulfillment of one's heart desires?"

Answer: All asked from the heart will have fulfillment. Hold ever to the Star of Hope. When least expected, it will be. Feel, think and know you ask not in vain. To waver in faith is to prevent the coming forth. Do not waver. Yet in thy desires ever say, 'Thy will be done, not mine.' "

Question: "Is it right to ask for abundant supply?"

Answer: "It *is* right. You have, even before you ask. Be aware, thus will your cup be full and running over."

Question: "When will poverty disappear?"

Answer: "When poverty is erased from man's consciousness. When man realizes the riches of Earth and Heaven are his."

Question: "Why, O Master, is there so much illness?"

Answer: "Alas, cause and effect is the answer to all life's troubles. To be clear of such, one must be at one with the Father, nature and man. This may take many incarnations, or man may be healed in the twinkling of an eye."

Question: "Can negative karma be liquidated quickly?"

Answer: "Absolutely. As one's faith, so be it."

Question: "Can chronic illness be healed, no matter what the disease?"

Answer: "According to karmic law, all can be erased and man come forth whole."

Question: "Can man achieve illumination without joining an outer school?"

Answer: "Yes. All depends on the inner development of one. It can be dangerous unless one is guided by a Master, visible or otherwise. Yet it has been done, and will be again. But it is advisable, no matter how advanced, to join an authentic outer school or order, even if one doesn't need such. It is splendid discipline and one may commune with people of all walks of life. Dare, do and be silent, is the law. Let your love flow ever from the heart, that you be protected through the dark night of the soul. Embrace nature. Become a good human and be dedicated to thy Creator, for without Him, thou art nothing."

Question: "Is it necessary to read the Bible to gain illumination?"

Answer: "It is well to read all sacred books, for all are inspired by the spirit of God and the Masters. All say the same truth in their own tongues. Yet still more important is to be able to read from Akasha and the Book of Life and nature and the heart of man."

❀ Chapter Six

THE MASTER H came in the evening dusk. Came he as I sat by the river bank. My heart lighted up like a thousand lamps. Soft amber haze silhouetted the atmosphere. I felt I was on holy ground.

"Pensatia, scribe of my books, listen well and write."

So spoke H to me.

"Within all nature lies the above, and in the above is all nature. Love of man for woman and woman for man is in the above, as it is here below. True affinities gravitate on earth and in heaven, each to the other. Many lives spawn the meeting of two souls. Naught can keep true love from union, one with the other. Early or late, the Creator brings together the Cosmic and earthly complement of woman and man.

"Come, Pensatia, put on your travelling cape, and swallow the green pellet. We go."

Even as he spoke, I obeyed. We lifted our Body of Light and with the swiftness of eagles were transported to a green and hilly dell. By a sparkling rose-pink fountain, spiraling from the Most High Mountain, I beheld a stream of men and women in pairs, walking in pink radiance and fusing as one.

It was beautiful to behold. Their soul bodies were luminous. A golden veil covered them and music of the spheres played a wedding march.

"Two souls as one," echoed the words from the Master's voice. "Here and here alone do true mates meet and wed. All in some life must enter the Path and partake of the Alchemical Marriage. This must be done by one or the other. If just one has been initiated into the spiral of the Rose Dew, the other will be drawn to him or her as a moth to a flame; for Cosmic law proclaims: 'All who attain the Alchemical Wedding shall also wed their own on earth.' Even though all seems naught, even though earth barriers separate, yet as a rainbow after a storm, they meet and know and two hearts become one.

"You are seeing the rare and mortal mating of man and woman — pure and out-giving like the sun. Seek only this love, all who read. It alone is true."

We left this panorama of Cosmic splendor. The Master stayed closely as we came to dark, ugly red caves and black night. Here we sensed and saw depravity and orgy. Saw we men and women, youth partaking of drugs, illicit sex and hate and coarseness.

"You are seeing the Cosmic reflection of what is taking place on earth."

A faint beam of light drifted down from the High Mountain and a few saw and arose and started on the upward Path. And the Star of Hope shone down.

"Look up and change your status quo. Decadence is settling over the land. Smother it out ere the stench destroy all humanity. Let Light guide you. Look up and aspire to the heights. Thus only can the tide turn and the Aquarian Age bloom.

"Come away. We go back to the river bank."

No sooner said than done. I arose and went inward to my room. The Master had departed. Yet the Star of Hope flooded my coming slumber. I heard within my heart the Master's voice saying, "Fear not, Pensatia. Man will yet redeem himself."

And peace profound covered my sleep.

Again came morning bright. Came song of bird and waking breezes. And from my heart's consciousness, Master H did speak.

Pen in hand, I record.

"Is God dead? No! It is man who is dead. Like a wild, untamed beast, he walks the earth, a slave to maya — to the passing caress of the flesh. Drugs, aye, dope, take the place of seeking wisdom and their Creator. Yet God ever sees and lets man go so far. Then He steps in and the will of the Father-God proclaims the Word: *'My will be done — not man's.'*

"Come ye out, O man, or the Aquarian Age you will not see. All who defy their maker and say, 'God is dead,' will behold the power of the Lord, for the kingdom of heaven must be on earth, even as it is in heaven. The harvest will be not in vain. The wayshowers of the Path — the light of their victory will sweep the world!

"A leader even now is wending his steps down from the High Mountain to touch this earth chaos with the Star of Hope. The masses will harken to his words. The avalanche of Light of Aquarius is pouring down to earth. All must be aware of its floodlight to survive. Faith must turn to a knowing. Reality comes with feeling. The Flame of the Heart will bring forth the birth of the Christus within all men. Womanhood will arise and reflect and give of their divine qualities. Thus will their love lift man to his Cosmic role in life. Nature will renew itself in its simplicity and pro-

35

foundness of reflection of the Above. The sages will be reverenced again. Man will learn through the crucibles to make gold and give gold. The alchemist's dream will become a reality. All sacred books, the Bible, the Koran, the Bhagavad-Gita, the work of Swedenborg, Boehme, Jung, and Tao, and all not named will be revealed as one message. All will be levelled to the Creator's divine design for humanity. The chaos of this century will pass into the Light of the Golden Dawn. Mankind will be purged of the dross. America will rebound from its mistakes and blaze its Cosmic heritage out to the world. Yes, the power of the Almighty is at hand. Law and order will be, and all that is not of the Fiat of the Lord will not survive. The natural, honest purity of God realization will make green and happy the land. Brotherhood will be a sharing — a giving, a serving out to life. Such is the challenge, the call within man's heart to the Aquarian Age. Listen, man, and obey. Know out of the depths is born the Light.

"Now, Pensatia, look up," spoke H. "See the swirling Golden Flame of Isis unveiled, see the pink Dew of the Rose, feel the Love Ray from the infinite Source. Sense the coming footsteps of a new leader, a new Moses, to liberate man from his self-made chains. Arise, O man, and look up to thy Star of Hope. Follow it and see the Promised Land of a new tomorrow."

Even as the Master proclaimed, one felt the caress, the tender vibrations of peace, joy and fresh creativeness to come. Like great organ music, one was lifted in consciousness to Akasha's archives of man's unity with the Father. Even as I listened, I knew through man, God's will would be done.

Arising, I withdrew to earth vibrations. The Master drew his cape of white about him and departed.

✸ Chapter Seven

THE MASTER came as I sat and pondered. Birds sang in green fields nearby. Squirrels played among aged tree branches. The Master spoke as he became alive within my heart.

"Pensatia, man sleeps and knows it not. In idle pursuit of the objective only, his spiritual body dies from want of nourishment. Thus the few who are rising up the ladder to Cosmic Consciousness are crucified, scorned, stoned because of the inertia and ignorance of those who will not hear or see or feel the Path esoteric — that fabled Way of the Alchemists, those of the Rosae Crucis, the Lotus of the East, the Tao and the Buddhist eight-fold road, the Way of the Essene, Jesus, the Christed One, the Way of the divine Kabalist, Moses, and others. Alas, the Creator, the Absolute, the Good Shepherd, will not pull man up by his boot straps. Man, himself, must do that. Of his own choice he must turn to the esoteric Path which leads to the Most High Mountain of Cosmic Illumination.

"Hungry one must be for the inner wisdom. In wonder and with open mind, one must, step by step climb and conquer. One must obey the truth of the sacred Tarot from the Book of Thoth. One must hear the flute call from heaven's gong and learn through the crucibles to play all notes of life and transmute them into the note of the Golden Dawn, that glory above and beyond the earth sun.

"Behold with me, Pensatia, the great immortal Sun of Life. Come, don your travelling cape of white, partake of the green pellet of balance."

Once again we swept over the vast expanse of space. Up, up to the black and beyond, into the Temple of the Golden Dawn. There, in that "gold beyond the sun," we walked in the splendor of pure Love radiance. The Temple, simple

37

white with pillars reaching beyond the sight of man, stood before us. In all its infinite simplicity, it radiated in the splendor of the Golden Dawn. Light, beyond the conception of mortal man silhouetted it in the background. One felt the immortality of man. All life blazed out from the portals of the Temple of the Sun. Stripped was one from all shackles of earth; yet, one could see, feel and know the kinship of all nature and humanity.

"Behold, Pensatia," spoke the Master H at my side, "all the wisdom of the ages is recorded here, in the golden archives of Akasha. Herein come the initiated ones of the Book of Thoth. Here come the disciples and Masters of the Hierarchal Host to participate and bathe in the golden rays of the inner Flame of Gold.

"Those who reach here in consciousness shall be healed of all earthly ills. Only stay and work from the Flame, and slowly and steadily will you be regenerated in thy earthly body, even though thou must be purged of all negative dross. Only settle thy consciousness in this ray of Gold, and all will be. Yet remember — seek not to enter until the Master bids you. Initiated thou must be first, in Earth, Water, Fire and Air. Remember, and do thy work. Obey, and surely as the sun rises and sets, so will you, at the appointed summons, partake of this celestial Temple. Come, let us enter."

We walked into the golden splendor of a vast lofty room of such immaculate whiteness that we felt purified by mere entrance. Attar of roses wafted its fragrance, delicate as summer breezes throughout the corridor. At the far end, three high jewel-studded chairs stood on a dais of purple velvet; yet it was not velvet, but of Cosmic material not yet known to man on earth. Seated in the middle chair was a venerable Master, unknown by me. A salutation passed between him and the Master H. Two angels, tall in stature, tendered a transparent goblet of the Water of Life.

"Sip, Pensatia," spoke H to me.

Obeying, I did drink the fluid of the elixir. Even as I did, I found myself alone. H had departed. Only the Hierarchal Host was there. He spoke.

"Come closer, Pensatia, scribe of Master H."

I drew nearer, and all the vibrating force of his aura engulfed me. I felt my consciousness being polarized in a higher note, as if my perceptions were so clear I could see, hear and feel forever, up and down. My every lack, every fault, all my naked weaknesses and omissions stood out. I was stripped of all save the truth, yet I felt good about it all. It was as if hidden dross was released from my system. Like a giant wave, the Golden Spiral poured over and through me, cleansing, uplifting.

The infallible Master spoke not. He only watched. It was a strong and heady drink, this elixir; yet it had a steadying effect. I went with it, realizing that to fight its effect would only destroy my experience here in the Temple of the Sun.

Suddenly, between me and the dais of the Master, came mammoth monsters. Serpents and hideous demon-like faces reached out to destroy me. A black and bitter stench engulfed me.

Gone the golden luster. Gone the majestic presence of the Master. Gone the angelic ones. Gone the exhilarating effect of the Water of Life. A sickening shudder ran through me. Yet, within my heart, I heard Master H speak.

"Where is thy faith, Pensatia? Have you not faced these oppositions before? Fear not! Advance and walk through these astral creations. Hold aloft the Rosy Cross worn upon thy heart. If you yield, you will never finish this book or write of this Sun Temple. Advance, Pensatia, and win!"

The voice ceased.

The marauders already had their fangs out, ready to devour me into nothingness. Suddenly, with inner strength, I did arise, holding forth the Rosy Cross. I commanded, "Begone, in the name of the Christus! I will have none of you!"

Even as I commanded, like a puff of smoke all cleared. The Golden Flame covered me like a garment. I stood before the Great One, seated in the jewel-studded chair.

"Pensatia," he said, "stand and receive the diploma of Gold, proclaiming you have earned the right to record the books and your journeys with the Master H. Remember, all you record and experience is designed for you to learn and grow. Only because you were chosen long ago to write these books were you granted these initiations, that you might give back the Truth. Thus were you brought in contact with him, the one chosen to publish *all* said books. Such was the reason for your early trials and tests upon the Path. Now, alone, you have faced these things and won your entrance here.

"Ask not my name. Know me only as the Cosmic Initiator of the Sun Temple."

Now, he did lay his hand upon my head and spoke.

"Pensatia, long will be thy days and great thy wealth. Love will bless you. New books you yet will write. Thy health will come forth. Before spring flowers the land, new strength will be yours. That which ails you will be no more. He who holds your North Node will befriend you greatly. He, born of the Sun, will communicate and meet you. As in past lives, you will be reunited in this incarnation. The Defender will prosper, and great art and writing he will give to the world; and his marriage will be blessed and both will walk the Wisdom Path. My chosen one, E.C.B., will come forth in new spiritual initiation and publish all the works of H. Such will be translated into other tongues. Share and give love and write. Yet above all, be human. By your work I give the promise — your sons will prosper, and that which grieves you shall be no more.

"Now ask what you will, Pensatia, it shall be granted you this day. Think well, for what you ask shall be."

In silence, I pondered and spoke.

"Oh, great Master, my desire is written in my heart. I need not speak. I can only say, 'God's will be done.' "

A smile of magnitude and compassion swept upon the Master's face.

"Well spoken, Pensatia. I do know your desires, your hopes. I here say your deepest wish is granted you, never to leave you. Arise now and go back to earth loam. When I bring you here again, as I shall, you will learn and write what you experience here in the School of the Sun. Let me add: where you are now, two neophytes of the ancient Way live. Tell them, as they obey, they will find and know and receive the Master. Tell them not to be discouraged, but, step by step, to conquer. They will attain. Old souls, they are of Atlantis. Say also to L: Have patience. Even so will she be reunited with a past love. Look up and give thanks."

After resting in earth's green hearth, again the Master H beckoned I journey up to the golden Temple of the Sun. There, by the tall columns, he bade me farewell, saying, "If you need me, call within your heart." I turned to thank him. He had vanished.

The massive doors of shining gold opened. As I drew near, a peace and balanced poise was mine. In joy and serenity I walked again to the Master Initiator seated upon the jewelled chair of antiquity. In his hand he held a

41

scepter, or wand-like pointer. He raised it as I advanced.

"Kneel, Pensatia."

An eye bore down upon me from the vaulted ceiling, covered with astrological symbols. I was conscious that a mighty presence was watching me as I obeyed the Master's command. On purple cushions I did kneel before the Initiator. For a moment, weakness lay upon me. It was as if my life force was ebbing away. Remembering the Master H's parting words, within my heart I did call him. Even as I called, new strength was mine.

With his pointed staff, or wand, the Initiator touched my center of the Third Eye, then my throat center. I heard a click, and then a white light lifted the veil of Isis. All my senses bore witness to the Light. Yet, I was polarized in earth balance also. A new dimension of being was mine. The oneness of all creation flowed over and through me. Music of the spheres resounded throughout the Temple, and bells pealed.

"Arise, Pensatia," spoke the Initiator. "Your centers once before were opened by the Zen Master when you recorded the book of 'The High Mountain.' Now, again, they are tapped by the word of authority. In the later years they will be rekindled."

Now, handing me a silver key, he said, "Keep this and fear not to enter the various chambers of this Sun Temple of the Golden Dawn. Your awakened centers will guide you. Yet, ere you leave, drink of the elixir of the Waters of Life."

Doing so, holding the silver key close to my heart, I advanced down the long corridor until I came to a high door that appeared to be of solid silver. It opened automatically at the touch of my key. A grey-bearded Master was seated behind a large flat table with instruments and what appeared to be maps or charts. I felt I knew this Venerable One.

"Be seated, Pensatia. I know of your coming. Before you can explore further into the archives of this Temple of the Sun, you must know the esoteric chart of your astrological future.

"I am Nostradamus. Long ago, you were my pupil. Thus your love for astrology and understanding was ingrained in earlier incarnations. It was written in your map long ago of your destiny to journey with the Master H and record his words for humanity to read. Thus were your preparations and initiations severe. But you have come thus far with victory.

"Draw close and let me read your esoteric map of the stars for you."

With interest, I obeyed. Seated in a tall-backed chair of much comfort, I awaited the information he had for me.

"Pensatia, you have transmuted your mundane chart. You have liquidated much wrong karma. Now your cause and effect stems from your actions esoterically."

He pondered, looking over a map of astrological hieroglyphics. Lo, I beheld the Star of Hope shining bright upon the pages. A great calm was upon me. Yet I felt I was to have revealed to me words of graphic import. Looking keenly upon me beneath his shaggy brows, he stated:

"Know, it is a Cosmic mandate from the Creator that all must face and redeem their karmic chart and evolve to the reading of this, their esoteric map.

"Listen well, Pensatia of the Rose. You will have strength, wisdom and health to record this journey and others before your passing. You have progressed to your Star of Fortune. Mighty Jupiter, Neptune, Uranus and Pluto here in your esoteric chart proclaim that as long as you obey your Cosmic mission, so will the stars bless and guide you. Herein is shown a temptation to fall back into the illusions of maya. But you will not succumb, and will arise and complete your work here in the Temple of the Sun and beyond. You will now have love, transcendent and earthly. Your health will be of enduring regeneration. Even so, the Defender will come forth a new man. From afar, a fortune comes to you. Give, share, serve, for the earth groans for lack of the Wisdom of the Ages. Follow always the middle path of temperance.

"You now have tests of a higher order, which you will pass, as long as you follow the Way of the Christus and Tao. Before Christmas comes upon the land, a meeting and a knowing will be for you. You have passed your greatest suffering. Now comes your harvest, even so for the Defender also. Remember, all spoken from the Masters will be. Partake of the Cosmic medication and elixir. Never cease to pray, meditate and forgive.

"Pensatia, record not what is told you now; treasure it within your heart. When all seems naught, ponder on it."

With gratitude, I gathered his immortal message within. Never will it leave me.

The Master departed. I left the Temple lobby and sauntered through an archway leading to a wide and lofty room containing books, reaching high into the Cosmic altitude. A page in white raiment greeted me, saying, "Your order of admittance, please."

I showed him my silver key and was granted freedom to learn from these archives of Akasha.

Books that were — and books to come — glistened in their golden covers. Ancient, present and future works I scanned. The page walked with me, answering questions relating to this Cosmic library. I beheld all the great books burned during the Inquisition, all new and bright, on every subject from Atlantis and days of Mu, down to the present time. All were represented here.

"Nothing is lost," spoke the page. "All is here in this place of books. When one's Third Eye is awakened, one may come here at will and read therefrom. Here, come the disciples of the Christ to read their treasured journeys with the Master Jesus. Here, come the immortal writers of ages past to comment and commune one with the other. Here, too, will come the present disciples to do research and relay Cosmic Wisdom down to earth.

"Here, also, are the names of books yet unwritten. As one writes, all is recorded here."

Now I did see a circular stairway winding upward to a round tower-like room. There, a venerable Master sat within. Climbing upward, I again displayed my silver key.

"Seat yourself," spoke he. "I am the appointed Guardian. Here is recorded the Wisdom of the Ages. When karma permits, individually and collectively, I release that which man is ready for.

"All great art, inventions, literature, medicine is here for man to bring back to earth when he has earned the right to do so. From here, Einstein found relativity. From here, scientists discover cures for diseases. Cosmic writings are conceived and recorded here for those chosen to pluck the wisdom of the Masters down to earth. From here, artists contact the real and paint on earth the cosmic design. Here also are the books of Black Magic, resting on dusty shelves. Here, the masters of the Black Art come to ply their nefarious schemes. There — look and see."

In a dark alcove were seated the Black Masters, seeking out new ways to practice negative magic on those who tread the Path to the Golden Dawn. Yet, they must stay in their own confines. They cannot enter the Light of the Golden

Library or the presence of the Guardian of the Light. In time, they die of their own poison. Yet, as all positive and negative is etched in Akasha, they try to ply their influence on weak disciples not grounded in the Rosae Crucis or the Lotus of the East. Having no desire to witness further this dark side of White Magic, I turned away. Amber haze softened the brilliant Light of Gold.

"Why not easy chairs for one to sit and revel in?" I asked the page, as I walked down the spiral step.

The page answered, saying, "It is Cosmic law that all who reach here in consciousness stand as they find, and return to mundane soil. Here, one transmutes to earth level, that such be shared with those ready for the Esoteric Path."

Leaving this Library of Akasha, I thanked the page and returned to earth vibrations.

In another chapter, I will resume my travels in the Temple of the Sun.

❀ Chapter Eight

AGAIN the Master H came in the silence of my heart. Came he and bade me don my travelling cape of white and partake of the green pellet.

"I go not with you, Pensatia," he said. "Fear not — you will be transported by your silver key. Search and record, my scribe."

Obeying, and holding the key of silver, I passed swiftly through many planes, up to the golden Temple of the Sun. All was silence as I walked through the noble architecture of golden splendor. A holy calm was everywhere, yet the presence of infinite Love overshadowed my steps.

Suddenly, I walked into the "Isle of Samos." Tall trees and grassy green slopes greeted me. My page was standing beside a running stream.

"Seat yourself here, Pensatia," he requested, "where you have been before. Know, Samos reaches into the Archives of the Sun. Here is recorded the Star of Hope, from the Tarot and the Book of Thoth. Now, look upon the running Waters of Life."

As I did so, I beheld the gleaming Star of Hope.

"Bear this image within your heart, Pensatia. And all who reach thus far, when low, and all seems naught, kindle within you this vision and reality of the Star of Hope. Ever look to it. Let its Christ luster lift your faith to victory. As you do, so will victory be through all adversity."

I absorbed the age-old symbol of Hope, and turned to the page. Lo, he had departed. In his place was the blessed Master H. He smiled.

"Pensatia, here we will relax and interpret what you have so far witnessed."

A serene calm settled over Samos and penetrated our beings. The Master spoke.

"Remember, Pensatia, and all who read: Clear sight, wisdom of the esoteric, are always revealed in the silence of the within. Here in the Temple of the Sun, of which in the far mountains of Peru is the earthly replica, all the secrets of the Love Ray of the Golden Dawn is, and will be revealed to man when ready. Knowledge beyond the ken of man glows in Akasha's archives. In the Aquarian Age all this will bloom for humanity's good. Yet man himself must seek, and through the esoteric Path, awaken his dormant chakras and spiral upward to the Creator's Temple of Light. The precious jewels therein are of such shining splendor, earth jewels appear dull in comparison. Yet, one obtained here and carried back to earth brings immortal luster to those of mundane value. As above so below, as below so above, is the formula through all and every thing. Those who buy fabulous jewels of earthly make can never attain the Cosmic jewels of the Temple of the Sun without first discarding the earthly ones. To attain the Cosmic first is to have both. See, O you of moneyed purse, that you attain the Jewels of the Sun first. Thus will you live long and be blessed."

Long we sat upon the loam of Samos. The Master explained many things of esoteric wisdom. Soft shadows of evening brought twilight upon us, yet an infinite glow as of cathedral candles cast an aura over Samos. The Master rose.

"I go now, Pensatia. Follow the page and sleep this night in the Temple of the Sun."

I turned. The page was standing close by.

"Come," he spoke. "You will sup and sleep in four-dimensional altitude."

A natural wonderment drew me on. We came to a simple rustic cottage amid wide-limbed aged trees. Strange exotic flowers bloomed without. The song of birds echoed through the tree-tops. Clean fresh air of rareness made the night pleasurable. All appeared solid and stable, yet there was a vibrancy, a scintillating lightness, which made it apparent that all seen was of a different dimension than earth green. I adjusted quite easily. Standing in the doorway was a tall personage. He held out his arms to me.

"Welcome, Pensatia! We meet again!"

I was most happy to be greeted by a teacher, who was a high rank initiate, and who had not long ago made the transit to a higher consciousness.

"Come and sup with us, Pensatia," he said. "Here on the loam of the Sun Temple and amidst the Isle of Samos,

I reside in this simple lodging. Here I meet my fellow Hierarchal Brethren. We have read your journeys with H, and have seen your lacks, your health karma, and the unfulfilled desires of your heart.

"Know, that which ails you will pass. All your works still unpublished, shall now be, and also those to come. Hold ever to the Star of Hope.

"How is the Defender? Tell him I am his friend forever. By reading this, he will know who I am. I will aid him in his work. Let him not forsake the Path. He has a spiritual destiny to fulfill, brought over from past incarnations.

"Pensatia, I passed to my abiding place here at the appointed time, which I foresaw. Come, let us step inside."

Within the cottage a familiar Early-American atmosphere greeted me. My friend joined a group of six other Masters who were already seated around an oval table. A soft blue light glowed through the golden haze, and the hum of music of the spheres gently touched our hearing. A rock fireplace was kindled with the eternal heating flame of the Most High Mountain. The table was set with snowy white linen and damask napkins. Pure silverware was laid beside silver plates; silver candles were lighted. A crystal goblet filled with the Elixir of Life was at each place.

At the table where the seven Masters sat was an empty chair. My friend bade me be seated among them. As I did so, I glanced up and beheld the beloved Master H and Alden of the Rose looking upon us.

Seated in the midst of these exalted brethren — all of them Masters who had trod the Way and won — the realization came that this was a momentous occasion; but for what purpose I did not know.

Then it was the tall Master at the head of the table arose and, with open palms, recited the age-old blessing of the

Rosy Cross, after which we, as one body, lifted our goblets of the Elixir of Life and drank of the bubbly water esoteric.

A new consciousness filtered through mind and body, a Holy Communion took place. The white Dove of Peace settled upon the venerable one. He turned. His penetrating eyes bored through me.

"Pensatia," he said, "you are here to bear witness to our meeting in the Temple of the Golden Dawn here on Samos. But first let us nourish ourselves on fourth-dimensional essence."

At once, there appeared fresh crisp leafy salads, green vegetables, as though just picked, and other savory dishes, and a rare wine, delicious beyond compare.

"As you see," spoke the tall one, "all is intercepted. Under the Law of the Sun, the higher Cosmic laws are used. The divine essence is transmuted to edible form. It is not gross matter, but the subtle essence of Cosmic manna.

"Eat and enjoy, Pensatia. Give thanks for this heavenly food."

As I obeyed, an influx of regeneration took place. The candle glow, the soft amber haze, the blue aura of the immortal flame burning in the fireplace, the rarefied air and the scent of attar of roses made the atmosphere most magnetic.

When we finished, all was cleared by unseen hands. The table was smooth. Only the glowing candlelight shone luminous upon the antique wood. Alden and the Masters had departed, even my old friend of Earth. Only the Master H and I remained.

"Pensatia," he said, "you were transported here to bear witness to the meeting of the Hierarchal Seven, and to test your ability to partake of the high vibrational essence of Cosmic food. Every particle of such bears the Golden Ray of Love from the Sun Temple. Unless one is soundly balanced, the food is too potent. All who are unprepared cannot eat thereof. Let me say you passed the esoteric ritual with honor and obedience. You have the permission of the exalted Seven to journey onward and record your further travels with me.

"Behold! Look upon your silver key! It has now turned to pure gold, with the purple Stone of Authority mounted upon it."

Indeed, it was so.

"This key," he continued, "will make possible quick attunement with me at any time. Yet use it only in your work and in earthly crises. Command in the name of the Christus and it will be.

"Remember, Pensatia, all given you from the secret archives are for you to ponder on and learn therefrom. Be true to your work and privilege.

"Now, go to the Field of Ardath and sleep as you have before, and may you awake refreshed and kindled anew spiritually."

He then departed.

Alone on a vast field of green and golden flowers, a drowsiness came over me. As I sank upon the yellowed bed of bloom and green grass, a peace profound was as a benediction. The resounding music of the spheres rolled over and through me as I fell asleep on the Field of Ardath.

It seemed long, my slumber. Age after age passed in my dreams. Life after life in panoramic pictures, from the primeval to the now was revealed, showing my upward progress, as well as my mistakes — my inertia. Revealed were my karmic lessons, both positive and negative. All was etched before me as I lay in quiet slumber. Also, the sweeping wave of the Water Initiation poured over me in its cleansing infusion. Felt I the Fire of Isis burning away age-old negations. Felt I the shackles and sorrow and pain of maya falling away from me. Like a sharp knife, the Sword of Justice cut away all false illusions.

Now, in my sleep on Ardath, was felt a mighty wind. I came to the Bridge of Light. Fear kept me from crossing over, yet I knew I must. Darkness rolled down upon me. The howling winds, like scowling demons, sought to lift me from my task. With all my strength, and holding to my key of gold and purple, I did place my feet upon the Bridge. Lo and behold, the winds became still.

I heard the Master's words. "Walk on, Pensatia. You will make it as you did before."

A consciousness prevailed that all experienced in slumber was indeed an initiation. Truly, the Master had guided me over the Bridge of Light.

I awoke standing by the great doors of the Sun Temple. Master H greeted me.

A new dedication to my work, a joy of body, mind and soul — like Cosmic music — poured through me as he spoke.

"Come, Pensatia, let us again relax in the grove of Samos and commune on the esoteric and the earthly."

We sat in the shade of the forest of Samos and talked of many subjects. With keen interest I listened as the Master spoke.

"Pensatia, wisdom is simple, yet profound. Though often veiled in mystery, it is plain to those who pierce the literal meaning. All esoteric books must be read from the heart. Intellect alone cannot open the door to the wisdom of the Rosy Cross. Franz Hartman, Jacob Boehme, Walt Whitman, William Blake, Emanuel Swedenborg — all bore witness to the Cosmic Consciousness of the Soul. All revealed the same kernel of experience expressed in their own tone and role of effulgence. To understand and reap the benefit of such books, one must go to them with a dedicated purpose; one must bore into the very soul of such. One must read again and again and ponder and seek to understand with open heart and mind. All must pioneer into the esoteric wisdom recorded by those who have been witness to such. Thus only will one feel and know the inspiration of the initiated and be led to the Most High Mountain of Cosmic Light.

"To have and treasure these immortal writings of the sages, is a privilege beyond compare. They bring blessings to you and yours, for each contains vibrational light from the Golden Dawn and adds vibrancy of aura to any room that holds it. So Pensatia, and readers, ever obtain the ancient mystical books of exalted wisdom, past and present, even though you may have to sacrifice for such. Remember, every authentic esoteric work bears the inner signature of the Hierarchical Masters and the Light of the Christus and the Golden Dawn. Though perhaps at first reading understanding may not come at once, one will feel it. Persevere, read and ponder, and you will be guided to the outer portal of the Golden Dawn or Rose and Lotus. Nothing comes to you — person, book, or the Path — by chance. All is earned by past or present cause and effect.

"A great love for people, for nature and for animals, must be awakened in man's heart as he hearkens to the call of the Mystic Way. A great forgiveness must go to all. When derided, and the negation of the ignorant seek to tear down one's steps toward the High Mountain, one must ever reach out and touch with love those who seek to destroy.

"The reason so many fail to attain the effulgence of the

53

Golden Dawn is, they are sincere, yet dry, and bring not joy and laughter to their task. They look upon it as a duty, rather than a service of dedicated love. They steep themselves in the letter, rather than the spirit. Their faith is weak. When all goes well, their faith is great; yet, when trials, tests and negative karma beset them, and all earthly props drop away, they become bitter and fall into maya again. Thus it is they cast away that which would carry them through the crucibles.

"O you of the Rose and Lotus Path, you who have started the journey to the Most High Mountain — do not thusly. Walk on in joy and faith. When all mundane maps fall away, arise and know, *the Masters are, God is*. Look to the Star of Hope to guide you on. Persevere! The Golden Dawn will be. Pioneer within yourself and find the key to the Bridge of Vision. Welcome every earthly loss as a gain to the Finished Kingdom.

"Pensatia, know, when Christed, man reflects nature and nature expands and glorifies the Creator. Sunlight and surging winds play over land and water, praising the Lord of Lords. Yet man, in beastly hatred, lust and rampage and anger, fosters the wrath of nature upon humanity. Nature appears shamed at man's downfall. Some day the lion and lamb will lie down together, as stated in the Bible. All nature will bless man and lead him. No longer will man destroy nature, but preserve its beauty and earth grandeur. Harken to my words.

"To destroy trees, flowers, and to pollute the waters of the Earth is to destroy one's self. Remember, O man, and obey.

"Neptune and Uranus have entered another astrological sign for twenty-eight and fourteen years. Here they will bear anew the message of the Aquarian Age and eliminate the weaklings who seek only the allure and shackles of maya. Embrace their Cosmic inspiration and go forward into the New Age. Seek to bloom the Rose upon thy heart."

Now the Master H arose, saying, "Pensatia, return to mundane soil and rest. In the next chapter we will talk and journey in further vistas of consciousness."

❀ Chapter Nine

SPOKE the Master H from the inner silence of my heart:

"Pensatia, here in the ninth chapter of attunement, I want to speak of action. According to Cosmic authority, often action is non-action and non-action action. Real action, remember, is orderly, and peaceful in wisdom experienced; it is not the spurious agitation of mundane intellect. *False* action often is like turbulent storms; it scatters, diffuses much wind and produces chaos. *Real* action is often accomplished underground, working with Cosmic law, not caring for world acclaim, but only for results for the betterment of humanity and the spiritual evolution of man's consciousness. Thus, working from the Center, such men produce action sired from Cosmic vision. These men are and will be the true Leaders of Action.

"Spurious action, individual and collective, is sired by ignorance and political degradation. Only spiritual integrity, faith and love of mankind brings true action. Remember, O man, and learn. Set afire your light within your heart. Then speak and act, not by might or preaching or loud reciting of big words, but by the very warmth and sincerity of the wisdom you have acquired in the crucibles of the alchemist.

"Remember, in the deep silence in one's heart is ignited true action, spawned by the Soul. Often, incognito, the greatest action prevails. The man who walks by the side of the road, a friend to man; he who brings laughter, love, understanding to those who pass by; such, by their very presence and walk are true exemplifiers of action. Action is a strong steadfast flame and servant of the Most High endowed with the Sword of Justice, with mercy and wisdom its guidance. He who has it blazes new frontiers and unites his action with the will of the Creator and the Hierarchical Masters.

"Action must be dynamic, positive; yet ever tempered with modesty and kindness. It must be the outcome of inner solitude, of soul nourishment and vision, which gives out to the chaos of today the Cosmic solution for the liberation of man and the sustaining of America's foundation. The true leader of action must first be a disciple of the ancient Path of the Essene, the Christ, or of that exalted initiate, Moses of Kabala wisdom. He must be a man at one with nature's secrets, a great human, one who humbly knows and walks with his Lord.

"Such a man will come. Already his footsteps are drawing near. Like a Lighthouse of Hope, he will, in the majesty of the Golden Flame, bring forth the Golden Dawn of Aquarian brotherhood. Only the Cosmic illumined man can bring peace to the world and silence the fires of war.

"Not by bombastic action or loud mouthings, but by an inner radiance and power of virile strength and warmth and love of heart will man stir and lift the shackles of his ignorance. Only a leader of health, vigor and authority will lead the world to light and awaken the people to the meaning of life. *Such a man will be.* Already one feels his approach.

"All actions of worth are generated from the womb of

silence; then, when ripe, are birthed out to life to fulfill their place in destiny. Remember, you who read and listen, enter the esoteric Path, that you also may become a man of true action."

The Master ceased speaking. I relaxed and pondered on his words. I then asked: "Tell us of old age, and how to meet and overcome it."

H smiled, saying, "Pensatia, old age is a myth. Embrace it with love, humor and inner vision, and behold, it disappears and *only life is.* As each season is ever new and ever fruitful of Cosmic Light, so each age of man is ever creative and flowing anew. Only man destroys the eternal spirit that lives through all the cycles of man. To become victorious over age, man must know the law and exemplify it. Light, Life and Love must ever prevail, and thus will one's body grow ageless, for the Body of Light will take over and be captain of the physical vehicle.

"Age is a reflection of man's stagnation, his negation, his lack of vision and failing to be creative and a lover of nature. To overcome the myth of age, one must be outgoing, giving warmly and attuned to the Masters and the God of all. Not in orthodox fashion and inflated ego, but by living naturally in temperance and joy, walking the middle path. All is relative, all is vibration. All supply, all life is of Cosmic gender.

"Age is not in spiritual latitude and dimension. Man must realize, 'as he thinks, so is he.' As man keeps his spirit, heart and mind young, so will his body reflect the light within.

"It is true, man's past karma often enslaves him. Not until he redeems it is he victorious over all. Yet this can be done instantly by realization of the change of our attitude. As the blood circulates, so must the Spirit of God circulate through man. Only in this manner can age be overcome.

"The way of the High Mountain, not the way of all flesh, is the way to remove the myth of old age. Remember my words, O readers. Learn the way of the Masters — the way of Noah, Abraham, Moses and the Prophets. Let the Christus be born within you and work and live from the Finished Kingdom."

Now twilight and hush of day's end called me to earth dimensions. Yet, alive lingered the words of the Master.

After a night's sleep I awoke to a sunny daybreak. Following breakfast, I settled down in reflective meditation, lifting my consciousness en rapport with the Master H. Came he down from the High Mountain, down from the Temple of the Sun.

"Come, Pensatia. We travel again to the citadel of the Sun Temple of the Golden Dawn."

No sooner had he spoken than we were there, transported in our bodies of light. We were greeted by a radiant woman in gold and white raiment, whom I recognized as the Cosmic and mundane mate of the Master — the beautiful Master Margaret with the deep black hair and dark soulful eyes.

She greeted me warmly, saying, "Pensatia, we meet again. You will come with me."

A meeting of the eyes, portraying pure love, passed between them.

"Pensatia," H said before he departed, "listen, learn and record words from my beloved."

Thus with Master Margaret I entered a beautiful garden retreat, of a silence and peace so tranquil it was as if suddenly we were freed from all turmoil of thought and action, as if we had stepped into the abode of a supreme and unknowable presence. There was a fountain spiraling up with sparkling waters, which threw out magnetic vibrations. The

58

ground was covered with green thick grass and lofty trees shaded the luminous golden rays. White lilies and lotus bloom grew nearby. Music, soft and low, resounded, accentuating the profound quiet of this garden place.

"Pensatia," spoke Margaret, "let us relax on this velvet green of grass and devote our stay here to thoughts and questions whose answers are written in Akasha."

I sat, quietly intent, leaning against a large tree.

"Behold, Pensatia," said Margaret, "from the fountain of the Waters of Life is seen the Living Rose."

A gigantic cross formed within the spray of the essence of the Waters of Life, and within its center bloomed a rose. Now I beheld a multitude of people bathing in the ever-flowing stream, and all bore a rose and lotus upon their hearts.

"What means this?" I asked the beautiful Margaret.

"It means," she answered, "all who attain the Living Rose and are freed from maya must bathe in the eternal spiraled fountain from this Temple of the Sun and the Most High Mountain. It may happen in sleep or in objective consciousness, but happen it will when the student is ready. One of the Masters will guide the disciple through the esoteric initiations. In the spiraled fountain of life everlasting is contained the Elixir immortal. All who drink from it can never know death. To attain this lofty secret of the Sun Temple, one must discard all lesser things and travel alone to the Golden Dawn. That is, one must toil daily in the alchemical laboratory, transmuting all negation into the pure gold of soul consciousness. One must attain and bring forth one's Body of Light and become aware on all dimensions of being.

"Experience on the esoteric Path produces a gradual opening of the chakras or inner centers. Only slow, steady application and obedience to Cosmic law will bring the student into attunement with the Masters.

"As one travels the road, one knows for a surety of the guidance and presence of the Masters. It is a natural process. One works from within, then without, learning first to be a good human, and living naturally and lovingly at one with nature and man. Thus progress within and upward to the illumined Mountain of Light is made safe.

"Often your very own friends will dampen your ardor. Negative forces will seek to pull you back into maya's illusions. There comes great dearth of action. Inertia creeps upon one at these moments. Be still and know it will pass. Let thy faith rise like a mighty flame, and lo, the bluebird will sing again and you will be lifted anew in communion with God and the Masters. Pensatia, each time you meet the ebb tide with love and serenity of mind and heart, you will be fortified; it will be easier next time. Gradually one becomes master over all dark nights of the soul.

"Pensatia, back of the man-made chaos of world conditions live and breathe a phalanx of visible and invisible Masters. They ever are working for the saving and turnabout of mankind. They do not force. Man himself must make the decision. Yet the Masters know only man can destroy or liberate the world in this cosmic space age. The mandamus is written clearly upon Earth's arena. Walk with thy Creator, the Lord of all people, or perish in the karma of thine own making.

"*There is a Path.* Seek and find it within thyself and follow through to the Most High Mountain. Thus will America again bear the symbol of the Eagle and be the Light of the World."

"Is it too late to redeem our past mistakes?" I asked. "Is it too late to reclaim the true Cosmic values and reach out

60

for the Aquarian Dawn? Must all end in disaster, or will man choose the esoteric Path of Rose and Lotus?"

"As man decides, so can the tide turn," Margaret answered. "As we, nature and individuals, find and use the Love Ray of the Temple of the Sun and use such for the blessing of the world, so will wars cease and nature and man be at peace, one with the other.

"Now, let's discuss prophecy and predictions. Remember, as man turns and walks with the Father, the direst prophecies may be transmuted into the positive redemption of the Finished Kingdom. Thus man is the creator of his destiny; it is up to him. Yet there is a limit. If one persists against Cosmic law too long, then indeed the Lord God speaks and sweeps away the debris and man starts anew, realizing at last his divine purpose in life.

"Those who still cling to maya's illusions, to man-made religion, to the spurious materialism, must perish in their ignorance. Those who love much and walk with nature, those who forgive all, who have gratitude and a humble heart, these most certainly will find the esoteric Path and attain the Golden Dawn and the Holy Grail.

"The Creator did not create man in His own image in vain. The Finished Kingdom will be realized on earth. Even as in the past, civilizations have risen and passed away, even so now a new renaissance, a new dispensation is at hand. History will not repeat its destruction, but the Golden Dawn will lift mankind into attunement with God and the Masters, within their hearts. Also, the Christus will be born again, and Brotherhood and Peace will prevail. Thus will the Kingdom of Heaven be on earth. Nature will flourish and happiness, laughter and reverence will abound in all hearts. Pure love will foster all marriages and there will be plenty in all the land. This is the decree of the Almighty.

"This is the Golden Age — the Aquarian Cycle. Many things will pass away, but not the Living Word. Heed not those who bring spurious predictions. Live according to Cosmic law. Have faith, the Lord will not forsake thee. Run not hither and yon, but abide wherever you are; the Master will guide you. If a move should be made, obey if directed, not before.

"Yes, the world is changing. World karma is demanding a pay-up. Nature is calling a pay-check long overdue. Man must give back to nature what man has destroyed.

"All cosmic space inventions must be used only for man's benefit and earth beauty. This will be. The time has arrived when a leader will come forth, when all the world proclaims as 'Man' one armed with truth, honor and vision. Such a one will rule, not by violence, but by love, understanding and a dynamic personality. He will save the world from total destruction and lift America back into its Cosmic mission.

"So take heart, you who read my words recorded by Pensatia. Lift up your heart unto the hills. Rejoice, for the Lord is your refuge and strength. Enjoy the peace of the evening hum and walk among the trees and the woods. Listen to the song of life, to the cheering notes of birds. Enjoy the simple true things of life — true friendships. Read great books, be inspired by sea, mountain, desert and valley. Live with jest, laughter and love. Reach out and let the light of your soul touch all who pass your way. Do this and you will find peace and fulfillment.

"I go now, Pensatia. Ponder on my words and prepare for the next recording.

"Well done, amanuensis."

❀ Chapter Ten

IN THE DAILY toil of life came the Master H. Came he in the consciousness of my heart. Yes, amidst the everyday actions was heard and felt his gentle touch, his words of strength and wisdom. And lo, in that inner attunement, I knew "the Lord is my shepherd, I shall not want. Seek and you will find, ask and you shall receive." Even as I pondered those time-honored words, gratitude welled deep within me.

Clearly, the Master H spoke, "Pensatia, write my words to man." Thus I obey.

"Even as all storms pass into the embrace of sun and flower, even as wild winds are soothed by the lullabies of gentle spring breezes, even as day follows night, even so will man, through obedience and facing the crucibles with faith, behold and come forth a new man.

"It is written in Akasha, 'He who takes the esoteric Path and obeys will surely attain the Most High Mountain. He who seeks wisdom rather than the falseness of maya will surely walk and sup with the Masters. He who enters with mind and heart into the deepness of life will surely walk with the Masters and find the Stone and Elixir; the victory of illumination will be his.'

"So, Pensatia, and all who read, let the valley and mountain intermingle as you journey the way of the Rose and Lotus. Even as the nightingale sings through the night, so must one sing through the dark night of the soul. So must you ever look to the Star of Hope, luminous token of Faith, shining in your hearts, bidding you never to give up, but to ever walk the King's Highway to the Shangri-la of the soul.

"To understand the living words of the Masters, one must truly go beyond the intellect. Only the pure heart rays can penetrate the potent power of such. All Masters have

63

experienced the Sun Word of Life; all have been initiated in the Secret of the Sun; all have known the Alchemical Marriage and have transmuted the Crucibles of Life. Thus by Cosmic attunement they speak with authority as Brothers of the Third Degree.

"To the average man, the Masters are a myth, an imaginary fantasy, an escape into the abstract. In their self-induced ignorance and apathy, they go through life after life as the 'living dead.' Only when life shocks them into an awakening, do some arise and seek the Cosmic portal of the esoteric. It is then, if sincere, and the student is ready, the Master appears and guides one safely up the Path to the Most High Mountain.

"All words spoken or recorded, as by Pensatia or other scribes, are potent with power. The very light of the Master's aura, the pregnant print of his voice, the white radiance of his presence as he transports his thoughts earthward and out to the world in book form — all are ignited with light, life and love. Some have been healed, or their whole life has changed from the reading of such books. There is a calling to each which penetrates to the open heart of all readers. There is born an empathy with the Creator and the Masters, and even so with nature and man. Each sincere reader feels and senses a warm and close relationship being spawned by the intimate words of the Master. It is as if each word spoken is impregnated with love and living wisdom. To read and study these words from the Masters, one feels uplifted and filled with courage and zeal to seek and find the ancient Path of Realization. Every true occult book carries the same vibrational light. If it doesn't, it is spurious.

"There is that mighty Cathedral of the Soul, where one may attune with and enter the sacred Holy of Holies. There, in the peace of Cosmic altitude, one may be at home with

God and the Masters. There, one may ask and receive, seek and find. There, as one meditates and listens to the Music of the Spheres, little by little the wisdom of the ages is unveiled and one walks away refreshed and closer to nature and man. No man-made church can give what the Cosmic Cathedral has for the human heart. There, nature lifts up its greenery and blossom, its mountain peaks and the glory of pure running streams, and as one worships God in spirit and truth, so also one feels the kinship with all life. Only when man has this rapport with the Cathedral of the Soul can he find the blessings of earth churches. All the outward splendor of the Temples of Earth cannot compare with the glory and beauty of the Infinite Cathedrals.

"Man was created to live in harmony with nature, to build cities of beauty, to create art, music, mirth and joy. Man was created to love and hold sacred the sex force. Man was created to walk the earth in peace and love."

Now the Master spoke about *asking*.

"One already *has*. We only *ask* to objectify the reality of fulfillment. Ever say, 'Thy will be done.' Have patience. Never doubt. *That which one asks for will be, if written in Akasha.* Often it comes by grace, if past karma permits.

"Too often, Pensatia, one's faith is weak. One lets go, hence one's answer dies a-borning. Hold and all will be. When ripe, the berry will fall in your lap. The Horn of Plenty was meant for all. If one is not aware, how can the bounty be there?

"Arise, O Man, and greet thy Creator of many gifts. Always remember: That which was spawned in past lives must be redeemed if negative. Yet know the infallible law: Pure love heals all ills. *Praise and gratitude* are the fragrance which transforms the heart. Liberty is false that carries man to excess. Tightness of mind is like tight pants — it splits into nothingness. True happiness is a flower which never fades, yet blooms greater as you give it to others. Storms are necessary only to clear the dross away. All real aftermaths are our teachers. Laughter, humor are great equalizers and the signature of a true mystic.

"Pensatia," continued H, "ponder on these sayings. They are written in all tongues, yet if not realized in action, are worthless.

"Now travel with me to Nature as God sees it, and as it will be in the Golden Age of Aquarius."

Thus again we raised our Body of Light to lofty dimensions. We landed in a vast expanse of variegated growth of trees, flowering shrubs, ferns and all descriptions of plant life never seen as yet on earth. The air was fresh and filled with the aroma of attar of roses. The Golden Flame from the Temple of the Sun shone gently over and through this Cosmic signature of Nature. Birds of yellow, blue, green and purple plumage sang their songs. Sheep, foxes, lions, tigers, deer, rabbits, dogs, cats — all were at peace, one with the other. The wide-spreading trees shaded a silver stream through the Cosmic land. In the distance, purple mountains were silhouetted against the horizon, and one glimpsed cities most beautiful, representing harmony and peace.

"Ah, yes," spoke H. "You are seeing in Akasha the Divine Plan for man. As above so below, as below so above. That which is the mandate of the Father must and will be. Naught man can do will destroy the Finished Kingdom. He only destroys himself.

"You were transported here, Pensatia, that you might record that to which you bear witness. Here, Nature and the Finished Kingdom is observed in all its divine creation. Thus you see, all the glory of the Living Word will be re-

flected on earth, yet man must first transform himself —
and then the earth. 'Man, know thyself' is the first law of
the Cosmic."

As the Master talked, one felt the majesty of God's love
and the wonder of His divine plan for man. Throughout
the spread of pristine nature, and viewing the coming forth
of the Golden Age of Aquarius, one sensed the peace profound of the realization of earth reclaimed in all the truth
of the Great Architect. I sensed humanity walking in peace
and unity with God and nature.

"Yes, Pensatia," the Master H continued, "health,
wealth, love and fulfillment is the Law of God. Only man
himself creates illness, lack and sorrow. 'As a man thinketh
in his heart so is he.' Remember, and think positively.

"Come, let us walk through Nature as God created it."

Tigers and lions came to us, reaching up for a caress.
Perfect specimens of the animal kingdom — foxes, rabbits
and deer gamboled or grazed contentedly on the lush green
grass. Birds of varied colors sang softly. All through the
large wide-limbed trees the gold amber light beamed down
from the Most High Mountain. A hush prevailed. Attar of
roses drifted over the silver stream flowing by. The presence
of Ra, the Lord of all, the Good Shepherd, prevailed like a
benediction throughout this journey with the Master.

Suddenly, a clear consciousness burst forth within me. A
knowing ignited the surety that the Creator knows each and
all of us — our innermost desires, our mistakes, our love,
our compassion. Yet infallible workings of Cosmic law were
revealed in order and exact formula. Man must discover
this and obey. Then only will peace, joy and happiness be
for all humanity. That is what all the Avatars sought to tell
the world. But in blindness and lack of faith, man turned
away. Thus, today, the decadence and self-destruction of

the human race. Only by an about-face, personally and nationally, can we be regenerated and be ready for the Aquarian Age, now beginning.

"Now, Pensatia," spoke H, at my side "watch and behold."

Even as he spoke, the inner signature of Nature and cities to come merged into the Golden Dawn of the Temple of the Sun on the Most High Mountain of Azùl, and I knew the Alpha and Omega of Creation glowed in its purity, high on the Citadel of the Sun. Life, Light and Love were God's fiat for Man. It is fated that Men climb to the Sun Temple and there find life everlasting. Then the Rose Pen of Akasha flashed out these words, and were echoed by the Master H, and thus I record them.

"All Cosmic books, all great art and music, are sired consciously or unconsciously from the vantage point of the Sun Temple of the Godhead. All doctors of the future will heal through nature's herbs, through music, astrology and the bringing forth of the Love Ray of the Golden Dawn. Drugs will go. The whole man will be studied. Doctors will be dedicated and Cosmically called and Soul enlightened. This will be in the full Aquarian Age. The world will seek to exemplify Infinite Law. Marriage will be by the pure mating of Soul and Heart. Wonderful children will be conceived. All false birth control will be discarded. The Cosmic truth of birth control will be learned and mastered by Man himself. The divine meaning of love will be taught from childhood on. Man will realize also that supply is ever spiritual and is objectified only as man is aware of such. The Horn of Plenty will flow out for all, as man realizes Cosmic law. Divorce will be no more — each will know his own. The light of the soul will prevail and those mated by Cosmic affinity will come together and naught will prevail against it, for Love will conquer all. Age will depart from man's consciousness. Man will realize that life, consciousness and love are the antidotes for age, that every season of living has its generative elixir. So, humanity, walk bravely through the chaos of the present. Have faith. This will pass.

"Through the Masters' overshadowing and selfless service, the Land of the Eagle will come forth, purified and purged by its mistakes; again, its destiny will prevail. America will, in humble dignity and spiritual wisdom, be a lighthouse — friend and spiritual leader of the world. Russia will join hands as a spiritual renaissance burns high. Again the Living Rose will shine its age-old light out in white glory to all men. White Magic, the esoteric Kaballa, the esoteric teaching of the Essene, Jesus, will be reverenced and followed anew by the Aquarian survivors. Reincarnation will be known as Cosmic law. Astrology will be honored in all its truth and wisdom. All that is of value in the past of Nature and Man will be preserved and honored.

"Now, before projecting back to earth loam, I would discuss herbology from its Cosmic and divine purpose. First know there is a herb for every condition of man. Yet man must be prepared to discover and use the many herbs yet unknown.

"The Sages, eminent Rosicrucians, those of the Golden Dawn, the true Alchemists, bore witness to the sacred truth and healing qualities of herbs. Wise is the person who seeks the wisdom and health-giving power of herbs.

"As in all things, there is a negative and positive quality in herbs; too much or too little is not good for one. Balance in all things is the law. Also, by astrodiagnosis, one finds the herb most needed by each. Also remember in Akasha grows the Divine essence of all herbs. As one attains the Golden Dawn, one is eligible to partake of the inner essence

69

of those herbs — many as yet undiscovered by man. Herbs are far superior to drugs. Paracelsus knew this. Man is discovering great zest for research and the truth of herbology.

"Even as astrology, esoteric and mundane, will survive all the ignorance of the masses, so will herbology. Man is to realize that nature is the true healer of the Godhead. Mankind is beginning to know that the Sages knew what most people have yet to learn.

"Slowly, but surely, man is awakening from the sloth of orthodoxy. Much of the folklore of herbs is true, and was practiced by our forefathers. Yet, far greater discoveries of herbs will come forth in the '70's and on into the full Aquarian Age.

"Thus, it is imperative that we preserve nature — not destroy the essence of flowers. To have healing qualities, it behooves man to live in harmony with nature, that nature bequeath her secrets to those who cherish her. The Indians, the Incas, were rich in their wisdom and usage of herbs."

❁ Chapter Eleven

"Pensatia," spoke H, the Master, "in these closing chapters, it is my desire to leave with my readers the inner signature of Cosmic and earthly truths.

"Know, all truth comes from Above to the Below and flows pristine through the heart of man, for him to accept when ready. That which is gleaned and harvested from within man's secret flame of the heart has the seal of God and the Hierarchal Masters; also, it is the gate to the birth of the Christus in the temple of the thousand-petalled lotus. The heart and the head unite, and behold, the Stone of the

Sepulcher is rolled away and the Babe in the Manger is born again. To each esoteric student this birth must be. This is the initiation *all* seek. So know, O you who ponder on my words, this is the privilege God gives all people who seek and find the gate to the Rose and Lotus.

"The waves of Aquarius are stirring the sleeping centers to life. Soul hunger calls out to be fed. Heed the call, else starve and wither away into oblivion.

"Self-conscious realization of God and the Masters is inevitable in the Aquarian Age. Negation and passivity of action is and will pass into the virility of knowing and serving through dedicated inner wisdom. It is written in Akasha, 'All things are born through the wooing of God and the inner Sun, that golden Light back of the earthly reflection.' In the maturity of the Aquarian Age, man will discover the secret of the Sun. Then will man be truly regenerated and death be conquered. Only man bequeaths death.

"Arise, O man, and know life is the law. Within man himself is the power and wisdom to transmute maya into the Stone and Elixir. Seek and you will find, ask and it will be given you. God's promises never fail, even so the Masters'. Pensatia, speak and it will be.

"Let us now return to the Temple of the Sun, there to reflect, learn and be aware of the Golden Dawn of the esoteric journey."

No sooner spoken than done. We were transported by our bodies of light to meet again the Guardians of Wisdom and Higher Initiation. Once again, the Master H bade me goodbye at the Temple steps. "Go with God, Pensatia, and fear not."

The great gold doors opened for me, yet no light greeted me. Deep heavy blackness invaded the long wide corridor, yet I felt the presence of the Master — heard his words within my heart, saying, "Walk on, Pensatia; know even in the blackest night, shines the Star of Hope."

What peace profound of the Rosy Cross! I walked on through the dark corridor.

Suddenly I saw the glow from the Initiators' aura shining from the dais where before I had met them. As I approached, the middle one, seated in the tall massive chair, arose and bade me stand at attention. Something about the venerable Master seemed familiar. A warm memory was kindled in my heart, yet I could not place him. He smiled and walked down to greet me.

"Pensatia, disciple of long ago, know you not your old teacher in a past incarnation in far-off Greece?"

"Pythagoras!" I exclaimed.

"Yes, it is I," spoke he. "Long have I watched your many lives, including your present mission. I have followed your assignments and recorded your journeys with H. Well done.

"Fear not, all your physical weakness will clear up, even so your vision. All books written will soon be published, and read by many. He who serves with you will have the means to publish all. The harvest is breaking.

"Now you go to the healing room. There, you will receive that which you need, and that which is your due will be yours. A karma still lingering will be lifted. Your 'Star,' which soon you will receive, will bless you and bring you fulfillment on all points of the Triangle. Wear it with my blessing. That which was lost came to another, as though by a miracle, so grieve not. The 'Star' you have earned. Wear it knowing it is truly blessed and will draw health, wealth, love and long life to you. Have faith. Obey, write and live fully."

I thanked Pythagoras and bowed to the two other Masters who were seated on the dais. I bore to the East corridor which lead to the room of healing. The last words of my old teacher, Pythagoras, rang in my ears.

"Remember, Pensatia, nothing happens by chance. All is etched in Akasha. Your cross was destined to go to another. Yet also, did you not send for the 'Star?' Yes, *nothing happens by chance*," he repeated. "Cause and effect is the Law of Being. Even so was it meant that you and another meet. Remember also, eclipses hasten or take away. The bitter and the sweet are as one. Drink of both one must."

Long did I ponder on the words given me by my teacher of olden times.

Now I came to an open door, arched and flanked by tall marble columns, and found myself in a cloistered garden. Lilies grew wild in a clear stream. A muted fragrance of attar of roses prevailed through the air. A soft hum of the AUM echoed over the grassy loam.

Seated close to the lily pond was the Essene, Jesus.

"Pensatia, amanuensis of the Master H," spoke he. "Here, when ready, come those who need healing of leftover karmic conditions from past lives. Know, no prayer spoken in faith from the heart is unanswered."

Here in the Temple of the Sun, Jesus bore a silver flask which he dipped in the running stream where the lilies grew. He filled it with water, and blessed it.

He handed me the flask, saying, "As you believe and have faith and drink daily of this, so will you be healed. This will never be emptied. Drink as often as you will. It will do its work and give you what you lack physically, mentally and spiritually."

With gratitude, I thanked Jesus for his gift.

"Go in peace, Pensatia," he gently spoke, "and remember, all that troubles you will pass. That which you put out will not return void."

The Master's words sank deep in my heart. I knew they were true and that all who have faith and persevere in the crucibles will sometime reach in consciousness to this Oasis of Healing and receive the Living Water, blessed by the Master Jesus.

"Yes, in some manner, healing will be. So condemn not, nor judge. Forgive all and love from the heart. Thus will you attain the Most High Mountain of Illumination."

As I departed from the Temple of the Sun, the Master H met me and we returned to earth vibrations.

"Pensatia," spoke the Master H, "every step is important. All must be learned and exemplified in the loam of matter. Every bit of knowledge acquired from within must be put to outward use or it withers and dies. Circulation is a law of life on every plane, mundane or Cosmic. One must give to receive. One must feel to know. Cold intellect alone stifles the bloom of the Living Rose. To seek occult power, simple and natural, is the way to the Living Rose and Lotus.

"Only a true human, sincere and dedicated, can attain this noble goal — self-conscious illumination of one's divine self. Austere, the Path is. It stands alone, ever beckoning humanity to enter and follow up its spiral trail to the Golden Dawn. Its rocky road discourages the weaklings, yet, to the true student it is a glorious adventure — a challenge — a virgin pioneering into one's Soul. Truly, it is the Mecca of all those seeking the Holy Grail. From the start to the finish, one discovers the wonder and majesty of God's infallible laws. One becomes aware of the oneness of all creation. One walks into the arena of life knowing there is an answer to one's inner questing.

"One realizes from the start of his esoteric journey the over-shadowing presence of the Masters and the call of the Christus, saying, 'Come unto me, all you who are heavy

74

laden and I will give you rest.' A strange peace tells one he is on the right track. Gratitude wells within his heart that he has entered the Path.

"Yes, Pensatia, the real student, dedicated and humble, with open mind and heart, is ready to pay the great price for that inner wisdom of soul awareness. In faith and obedience he climbs the arduous road to Calvary and the resurrected Rose. The true infallible laws of the Path are obedience, gratitude and faith. Have these and no matter the crucibles, the tests, the neophyte will surely ripen and blossom into the disciple and, in some incarnation, the Master.

"Again I will answer some questions asked by the layman and neophyte."

Question: "Is not life the Path?"

Answer: "Yes and no. Let us say life reflects the Path when viewed esoterically. Life is the vehicle which spawns the Holy Babe when awakened within the heart and temple of the Lotus at the top of the head. The Path is in life and life is within the Path. Only initiation makes one aware of this seeming paradox."

Question: "Can not one attain illumination in the orthodox religions?"

Answer: "The answer is *no.* One must pierce the veil of the greater mysteries. One must partake of the inner mass within the outer. All forms of man-made laws must give way to the light of the Golden Dawn. All differences must be equalized into the oneness of the whole. All forms dissolved are straight lines transmuted into curves. Only the Cathedral of the Soul and Nature are the true Tabernacle of the Mystic Way. Only there are the cathedrals of earth justified and fulfill their mission. As above so below, as below so above.

"Pensatia, as I walk earth roads and pass through cities — as I contact the hearts of humanity — always I sense the hunger, the yearning for their lost heritage of soul consciousness. I feel the sorrow of their ignorance and would lift them out of their self-made bondage. But, alas, only they can make the initial start; only they can make the decision to enter the way of the Rose and Lotus; only they and you and you can open your heart and heed the call of the Most High Mountain.

"Yes, often a great sadness engulfs me. Why, oh why must humans bind themselves to the chains of maya?"

Now the Master arose. In strong, emphatic voice he spoke out:

"Man can liquidate all negation in a flash by instant dedication and service to the Christus within. Man can climb the rugged road to Calvary and there be resurrected. Man can transmute the crucibles into the pure gold and the elixir of the Alchemist. One can co-partner with Nature, using its secrets to make green and blooming God's Earth. Man, through the ageless Path of the Rose and Cross can bring the Golden Dawn to all those who seek.

"This is not an idle dream, but a Cosmic fact, sired by the Creator's infallible laws. This is not a fantasy, but the wisdom of the Masters.

"Goethe, Bacon, Brother Lawrence, Pythagoras, Paracelsus, Nostradamus, Franklin, Jefferson — all followed the Path of the Sages and left their immortal mark upon the Earth.

"Today, all may listen and heed the call of the Path now open in this Aquarian Age to all who truly search.

"Only by making an about-face, personally and nationally, can mankind find peace and brotherhood."

76

❊ Chapter Twelve

"Pensatia," spoke H, "my scribe and student of the Rosy Cross, and all my readers who have pondered on the recorded journeys of Pensatia with me, the time has come to write *finis* to this book.

"Much seems repetitious. So be it. Does not the sun repeat its coming up day after day? Do not cycles repeat themselves? Does not the good earth repeat its harvest — also the rains, the tides? Also, words of wisdom are read and written over and over. As man becomes aware, he rises in consciousness above and beyond the repetition, yet ever being renewed with its essence.

"The difference between a neophyte and a true disciple of the Path is that the neophyte, in ignorance and impatience, questions the need for repetition; he thinks he can jump at once into the solving of the Mystic Way. Repetition to him is a waste of words and time. Thus the reason so few stay to become disciples, adepts or Masters. The disciple honors repetition as a Cosmic law and fiat of the Creator.

"Until one can humble himself and seek and love repetition as a friend and teacher, he is not ready to progress. Yet know there is a spurious repetition that means nothing; such leaves the reader empty physically and mentally. It is for him to distinguish the substance from the empty shell.

"Also, these journeys may appear fantastic, even an impossible tale. Yet, believe me, the sincere reader will sense the truth of all written herein. There is felt an aura of light, almost a near presence of myself, which overshadows every reader. This is true.

"I, the Master H, live within my words to all who read. Yes, there are marvels of experience, glorious vistas, communion with the immortals of history in art and music. There is the scintillating magic of scenery beyond the pro-

77

saic splendor of earth. God's creative fiat for man is life and more abundant life. The ambassadors of the planets transiting the signs of the zodiac create the tides of expansion man needs to bring his rebirth to the divine goal of all mankind. Such is the Magnetic Light — the Word — proclaiming the living call of the Essene Avatar: 'I am the Way, the Truth and the Life.'

"Ever it is the spirit of the Holy Grail that makes possible the lifting of man's consciousness to oneness with the Father. Only through inner awakening can the Living Word be heard and obeyed. Know, the Word shines in man's heart; it is for man to bring it forth, kindling it in plant and animal life.

"So, dear readers, it is the desire and prayers of my Hierarchical Brothers that each and every one who reads will seek and enter the esoteric Path and know the Living Word of the Logos and hence use it to exemplify and to bring forth the potent waters of the Aquarian Age. Such is the mandate of the writing on the wall.

"It is not unique, the Path, but a simple flowing of man's being walking back to the Father, Creator of all. It gives no magic potion, no easy way; just the Living Word, the Holy Grail. The illustrious steps of the Masters, the disciples and the homespun people who give their all shine like glowing stars upon the Way.

"*The Path is.* Seek and find it. Enter. Learn from its eternal archives. Find that peace profound — the inner riches — that you may have earth's riches also.

"My words are recorded by Pensatia, a student who, by mistakes, falling and rising, ever obeying, is seeking to overcome, to attain the Living Rose of Life. Only by embracing the Living Word can and will humanity exemplify the Aquarian Light and hence find peace and brotherhood.

"Now I reach out to all who ponder and, with patience, seek the inner meaning of this book. To each, I touch in some manner the Lamp of your Heart. Turn up the wick, that creative vision may blaze out to life. Let the valleys, meadows, deep woods, the shining stars, the mirth of clean humor and love radiate these Living Words. Enter the Path. Obey the boot training. Dedicate your heart to the age-old Path of the Lotus and Rose. Thus will I call you and lead you to Cosmic and earthly fulfillment."

So ends this journey with the Master H. May I and all receive the Living Word.

So mote it be.

· · ·
· ·
·

The Path

DEDICATED TO CAROL

A Keeper of the Flame

Prelude

THE Master came. How, when or where, does it matter? Yet if you ask in sincerity, the answer is:

First, within the heart came he, out of that conscious rapport.

Silhouetted in Earth's reflection stood the Master H, wide-shouldered, strong in physical and spiritual aura. Thusly, wherever my self was, in city, country green, or mountain valley, or beside hearth fire safe from winter's cold, everywhere, all bore to me a golden flame, a generating feeling of peace and love, gently as a soothing lullaby.

Sadness and sorrow seemed far away. The whole wide world glowed bright within my heart. It was then the Master spoke, clear and direct, these words:

"Pensatia, my amanuensis and co-traveler, write now as we meet on that Path which is *immortality*."

Music, soft and low, as cooing doves sounded close to my listening ears. "So mote it be," I answered, ready to do his bidding.

He handed me again the pen of Cosmic power, saying, "Well done, Pensatia, you have spoken from your heart. We meet again soon. Live naturally until that hour arrives when I bequeath to you the first chapter of '*The Path*.'"

Fiery flame flowed through my being. A humble gratitude and a sense of responsibility for this, my assignment, was deeply felt.

May all pray that my recording with the Master be true.

PENSATIA

❀ Chapter One

"THE PATH," spoke H, the Master, is a state of consciousness man becomes aware of, when an inner initiation takes place in one's heart. It is then the Path is revealed as a reality. Until this happens, man is unbelieving that there is a Path.

"Even though one might be a member of the Rosy Cross, a Yogi, a Zen Buddhist, or a student of one or another of the various schools or doors to Cosmic attainment, many never prove the reality of the Path within. This is due to lack of endeavor to pierce the veil which hides the Path from those who have not earned the right to know the ancient mysteries. It is due to skepticism and materialism. One has not surrendered his all to seek and find the Path. Such ones, disillusioned and blaming life that they have not found, soon leave the outer portal, or school. They have not the fortitude or zeal to carry through the entire training required to discover the Path. They must have guts and perseverance before the Path opens for them. When one feels, sees and knows the Path, then all nature awakens for him.

"To be aware of this mystic way, or road, is to function fourth dimensionally, to come close to the divine signature of all life. Every commonplace experience or mundane duty takes on a new note. An aura of scintillating light, a celestial beauty, transforms all ugliness to a mystic fusion with God and the Masters. The forthcoming of the Golden Age is seen on the horizon. The seasons pour out their secret meanings. The dripping rain drops, the falling snow, the green fresh spring, the lush caress of summer's bloom, all is translated to a heavenly causation. To one who walks and knows the Path, the most common toil appears like a princely assignment. Until one knows there is a Path, one walks in spiritual blindness, in a dead world of earthly sight only.

The inner door is shut by man himself. The vitality, the Cosmic vibrations, the very essence of nature and humanity are blacked out by the ignorance of man himself.

"The Path, that blessed road winding through life's vicissitudes straight to the high mount of illumination, is a reality. While an intangible, to the initiated, to those tutored to see, feel and experience, it is an actuality of rare value. If God had not created this Path with the power of the Word, man could never evolve to Soul consciousness. It is through this Path and the Hierarchal Masters of the White Lodge that man finds the eternal secret of life everlasting.

"This Path is not found by wishing, but by a deep and lasting desire and faith and an inner search. The Path dips, rises and curves through the labyrinth of one's being and outward through life. It shines like the sun, yet is as dark as ebony. It is smooth, peaceful, yet stormy with waves of earth flowing through it. It is vibrant with the challenge to man to realize self-conscious immortality. It is never destructive save to those who seek to walk it for their own selfish reasons. The Path, Pensatia, is the only reality which never changes. All else is dual and illusion. Nature and earth manifestations when undiluted by man, reflect its Creator. Even though the masses are unconscious of the Path, still, like the Star of Bethlehem, it illumines all who are aware.

"The Path has ever been. Even back in the Stone Age it glowed deep in the cave man's heart. Now and then, one more receptive felt the leap of Cosmic Flame, and this became the forerunner of its birth to man. Thus age after age, the seed of the Rose of Life sprouted, and rays of light penetrated man's ignorance, pouring out its luminous light to man, starting his soul evolution. Now at the close of the 20th Century, and the emerging into the Aquarian Cycle, the Path is becoming a conscious goal. It shines within the heart, ever calling man to arise and follow it to celestial heights of initiation esoteric.

"On the Path man objectifies all his talents in service to God, the Masters and humanity. One realizes in truth that the Creator is the Shepherd of man, ever leading one beside still waters. All the wonder of life walks by his side revealing the creative love of the Cosmic Father. Even though the Path winds through all the sorrows and changes of maya, or earth lessons, secure in the peace profound of the center within one's being, one is master of all experiences. The Path is the summum bonum of life, the wayshower to Edenic consciousness with the Father. It is nature's revelation to man, the golden arrow to life everlasting.

"As we have these intimate talks and esoteric journeys, Pensatia, we will speak of the many aspects of the Path and how to distinguish the false Path from the real. For know, side by side, parallel runs the opposite Path of negation and death. Be not deceived by the glamour of the Black Brethren, those who seek esoteric laws for world wealth and destruction. Remember the true Path seeks atomic wisdom and discovery for benefit and healing of humanity's ills, not for war and killings. The negative Path speaks out boldly against all that is wholesome, pure and of Cosmic vision. It seeks only to enslave man by wrong thinking and acting, to allure him into the way of all flesh. It makes pleasant to the senses all glamour, yet ends in ashes and disillusion. Be discriminating, search within for the guidance to find the right earthly door to the citadel of the Living Rose. Thus will the esoteric foundation be started and the lesser and deeper mysteries unfold for you....

"Come, Pensatia, journey with me to the first inkling of the Path and on through to its glorious summit."

85

Obeying, the Master H did again give me my travelling cape of white and pellet of "balance" and we travelled upward with great speed on through the vast dimensions of space and on upward until we came to the glory of the golden Path back of the sun, which trailed to the earth, glowing sparks from the Godhead. This golden road as it bore earthward became mellowed and rutted in maya's duality, yet kept intact its Cosmic virility and its secret of immortality.

"Yes, Pensatia, back of the earthly sun is the esoteric Path of the way of life everlasting. The sages and wise men have known and followed the alchemical trail to Isis unveiled."

Even as he talked we were on that golden road which spread like a wide ribbon down to the world of humanity. Yet man saw it not, blinded by materialism and lack of faith. The Path runs parallel through earth with the Word flowing like molten lava down within the hearts of men and they know it not. It was true, we bore witness to the Creator's divine plan for man. The pristine essence of man's divinity glowed brighter than a thousand suns.

It was as if, and truly so, the secret of life poured over and through us, lifting our five senses to that light which lighteth the world. We felt no strangeness, only a radiant familiarity, as though we were in our rightful place. In that golden flame behind the sun, as we stood erect in the brightness of the creative fire, our earthly body was as though regenerated. We felt vital, our whole being responded to the alchemical transmutation. All the purpose and meaning of earthly and higher dimensions was shown in its naked splendor. Law and cosmic order was revealed in numerical clearness. Akasha's map of all spoken or lived was shown in the splendor of the heavenly sun. Our eyes were able to sustain the startling light. It neither hurt our sight or the other senses. We were aware of the AUM within this dynamic burst of light. We were conscious of a white stairway descending earthward. Amidst the golden glow the Hierarchal Masters walked to and fro and relayed their message down to earth through the ready disciple. The Word from the heartbeat of the Father sparkled like great diamonds. Those ready caught the Cosmic influx and sought the Living Rose. Master H standing with me spoke gently.

"Pensatia, behold the stairway all must climb. All must stand and face the creative fire of the sun. Only then can everlasting life come forth for man. The masses only know the outward mark of life. Thus death is the only answer. To live one must embrace Life not Death. One must seek and find the hidden flame back of the earthly sun, and bathe in its eternal Light. That is the Path, the vibrational glory we are standing in. Until man stands in this Light, which flows down into man's heart igniting that immortal spark, one will never have self-conscious realization."

As the Master spoke we perceived many persons from earth walking the stairs immersed in the brilliant golden flame. They carried the awakened consciousness of life's essence in their heart and its glow they exemplified out to humanity. Yet the majority, in ignorance, live satisfied, ever seeking escapism in false glamour, not realizing it is man who kills himself, not God.

In this golden Light we observed the most wonderful scenery — rivers, streams, mountains, vibrant with beauty and purity never seen in earthly atmosphere. "When man knows his luminous divine self, then indeed will earth reflect the 'Above.' All who pass through transition disciples on the esoteric Path, find fulfillment of their soul desires. God, the Creator, lifts the disciple into that infinite garden where love transcendent meets one. There, where earth pain and sorrow is nil, only the crescendo of life in its supreme essence meets one. Earth experience can not compare with the joy of walking the golden Path behind the mundane sun. There one moves and acts from the celestial fiat of the Word. All who know the Light, each in a different way realize their Soul objective. If one passes through transition without achieving the harvest of his heart's desires, rest assured the Cosmic Father bestows all in the Elysian land of the golden Sun. There one basks in the fruition of deserved laurels until one has the urge to reincarnate."

Now from the dimension of the golden Sun, where from the beat of God's heart the Path swirls down and through earth, was seen personalities reincarnating, seeking new birth in the material womb, was heard the first-born cry and birth of the living Soul. Standing with the Master on the Path of the Rosae Crucis, I felt the Holy Word vibrating through my whole being. It was as if Isis' Veil parted and liberated man was conscious of his divine estate. It was a marvel beyond human conception, this molten journey of esoteric light. All sensed was a steady feeling of the presence of God and the Hierarchal Masters. The Cosmic Hosts stood tall and straight in the Cosmic air. There was a humming wind, like music in the atmosphere, soothing yet stimulating, lifting one's thoughts to celestial heights. One was bathed in the waters of life. Yet this Path was seen winding through all earth lanes. It was inspiring. One knew Cosmic illumination was an invincible mandate for man.

"Yes," spoke Master H, "as above, so below. When one is awakened to estoteric wisdom, behold, one realizes earth is a heavenly paradise reflecting the luster of the Hidden One. In being aware of the Path, one takes earth's vicissitudes with fortitude, for he has that profound peace and stillness. Ever within him, in his heart consciousness, this eternal fountain brings joy to all trials of maya."

Now, as the Master H spoke, we perceived a jungle of fantastic growth. All was intertwined with confusion. A multitude of people seethed along, untutored, fighting their way through the chaos. It was not the verdant green of nature, but a sordid forest of man's negative creation. Yet viewing this panorama of cause and effect, man's self-induced karma, I beheld the winding sunglow of God's Lighted Path, and a few now and then saw, and stepped thereon, starting the journey up to the mount of Azùl. Here, on this Mystic Way of all the travelers, from Moses, Jesus, and the philosophers — Emerson, Lincoln, Whitman, Bacon, and the noted past Imperators of the Rosae Crucis, all reached down to those sincere seekers, or pioneers who dare to find the Master Path. With every step upon the golden road, man overcame his ignorance and caught a glimpse of a new life, spawned by the esoteric Path.

"When one is aware of the Path," spoke Master H, "and it is ingrained in his consciousness, very rarely does the dedicated student leave. And if he should, in Akasha is ingrained that momentous first initiation. Even though man may choose to depart from the Path, his divinity follows him like a glowing star from high heaven. In another incarnation he will reclaim his occult journey. The Path is the pristine print of man's pilgrimage to that Cosmic illumination which spawns the Stone and the Elixir. On this Path man brings forth his immortal self. Step by step the neophyte struggles upward to the celestial mountain. He learns that without the Path man groups like driftwood on the Sea of Maya. One realizes his relationship to God, nature and man. The whole future of the world rests on the foundation of this esoteric Path of the Masters.

"The Path is not in Orders, Cults or Churches, though they may be the door to the inner search. It is in man himself. In the depths of one's heart the Master comes and sups with the potential disciple. If one has braved and passed the boot training, then the Master aids in opening the chakras, and guides one softly through the initiations esoteric. Boehme, Brother Lawrence, Swedenborg, all the Avatars of past history, and unsung Cosmic heroes and Cosmic servants bore witness to the Golden Dawn and Rose of Life. Yes there is that transcendent moment of Soul Light when one knows there is a Path. Ever after, life has a profound meaning. Like green fresh spring, God's Love shines out to man, leading one to his immortal destiny: Cosmic Consciousness. When the Path is discovered the neophyte *knows* there is that High Mountain of illumination which all must climb and conquer. There is no guess work. One is aware from the first step on the Path that it is rugged, and even dangerous. Earthly dross and excess baggage must be left behind. Unless one is willing to surrender his all, the Path discards him automatically. Always man is given the opportunity to walk the esoteric Path. Whether one stays on it is up to the individual. No Master can interfere, or does, with Cosmic law, which is: 'Only he who earns the right may attain the Most High Mountain of the mystic Path.' Often, spurious ways are sought by those seeking to escape boot training and the arduous discipline. This always ends in disillusionment and often tragedy. Cosmic law is just, impartial and inevitable. The 'straight and narrow,' the long Path of the Sages bears no favorites, no crashers, no idle dreamers. It takes guts, obedience, humor, and an open mind, a dedicated heart, a childlike wonder, and faith in God. Have these ingredients and perseverance, and nothing will keep one from attaining the Holy Grail."

The Master now ceased. Holding his gnarled staff his gray square-cut beard shone silver as he bore upward to the heights of the Living Rose. His voice trailed back to me, "I will come again, Pensatia. Until then, let peace, love and faith be yours, and all who read."

❀ Chapter Two

Now I did walk with the Master beside the Sea of Maya with its ever changing moods.

"Be still, Pensatia," spoke he. "Tell me what you see, what you feel."

I obeyed. He turned and said:

"It is the ever-restless man in self-made slavery. His ignorance, you sense, Pensatia."

It was so. Yet above all, the hum of the AUM, the music of the spheres was heard. I saw man caught in the riptide of his karma, not knowing how to liberate himself. Yet I sensed the hand of the merciful Creator ever hovering over humanity, awaiting the moment when man lifts his consciousness to the illumined heart. Through the patterns of maya's ever-changing colors, I beheld the golden temple of Isis unveiled, its glow shining down from celestial heights and centering on earth. Behold, multitudes poured through its portals and light spread over the land. Heaven and earth awoke and knew their oneness with the Hierarchal Brethren. The Avatars, led by Jesus, the Essene, flanked the temple steps and spoke as in one voice.

"Thus is man's destiny."

Now the Master showed me the bitter waters and sorrows of the dark night of the soul, showed me the turbulent mirror of illusion which man gazed upon and thought real. As man sipped and sank into the darkness of ignorance, those who kept faith with the Alchemical Rose, those who meditated in the stillness, those sincere and pure of heart, traveled on. The Golden Dawn watered their efforts and their darkness passed into the glory of cosmic consciousness: man realized self-illumination. In the center of his being illumined man knew heaven and earth as one. He knew man was created to have paradise and the kingdom of heaven on earth. He knew life not death was the law of the Cosmic.

"The Path, Pensatia," spoke H, "has many alcoves, many resting banks. It carries the symphony of earth with it, up through its winding curve to the High Mountain. There, on its road, Kismet is met and one walks the 'Bridge of San Luis Rey.' There one experiences through initiation the Alchemical Marriage. And the Kundalini rises to greet the Risen One. When the Lotus blooms, when heart and head unite in one flame, man's chain of negative karma is broken — one stands redeemed. On this Path, the summum bonum of life is experienced, and wisdom of the heart awakes, and there, in service, all received is given out to life.

"The Path is the esoteric melting pot of humanity. Thereon, all have an equal opportunity to attain discipleship and mastery. Race, creed, etc. matters not. The Path is open to those who seek the wisdom of the ages. To these dedicated neophytes, all the keys of the kingdom are bestowed upon them, when earned. The Path is secure, molded in the Cosmic loam, fortified by the Living Word of the Logos. From the ignorance and darkness of earth, like a golden sun it reveals man's divine journey to the Shangri-la of soul consciousness. Only as man steps away from the Path does maya's illusion and duality touch him. The shallows, the pitfalls, have no place on the Path esoteric. Challenges yes, and a rugged climb. Yet always the trials are on the mundane level, the hurts, self-made negative karma. When the disciple has transmuted the chains of cause and effect and, through initiation, walks in the Light, the grace of God, the Master's love, protects him as a benediction. One is in the world but not of it.

"The common denominator is found in all people. The neophyte entering the outer portals of the esoteric highway must prove his right to every stratum of consciousness. Tested and tried in the crucibles, he comes out the divine alchemist having access to the akashic archives.

"The Path for every one is a personal spiritual initiation into man's Soul. When this takes place man is lifted into cosmic consciousness and infinite harmony with earth and humanity. It is a rare, sacred occasion this union with one's divine Self. It cannot be attained by spurious drugs, or delving into the occult, but only by utter surrender to the Christus and God. Beware, those who seek to open the chakras of communion with the Oversoul by drugs and false cults, which promise much, yet only lead one to disillusion! Beware of the glittering front, the smooth masters of the Black Art! Stand straight and tall in the simplicity of the Path, leading to the Mountain of Light. There on its sacred height man, by his earned discipleship, eats and sups with the Masters. Through the long dark night he has kept vigil and the high watch. He has come through the abyss of ignorance and in victorious mastery of his lesser self has resurrected the Rose of Life. Henceforth he is one with the music of the spheres. This beatitude does not come overnight. Years of discipline and dedication to the quest make possible the journey celestial.

"Pensatia," and now the Master H with all the sternness of mastership spoke. "The cycle is arriving when only the Path will be. All earth will blend into the Path, and the Path into it. The Golden Age will be. Now the Path is only visible and tangible to the initiated few. To the worldly masses it is non-existent, a myth, a fairy tale. Only when lightning strikes and man is stript of all worldly props does he search for the hidden Path esoteric within himself. This is not always so, but a common factor.

"Be it as it may, Cosmic law prevails, eliminating those not prepared for the inner journey to the Cosmic estate of man. When students keep faith that the Path is, even when as yet they have not experienced such, these pupils will know for a surety the Master and the Path. Faith at the outer portals to the goal is essential to illumination. Without this ingredient the Path is not witnessed by man."

Now the Master did gaze over the earth through the Lens of Heaven and he bade me look also, which I did, and all life's panorama shone with the golden aura of the Path. Man saw it not, for closed were his inner centers of communion and sight. Crusted they were with their objective faculties. Only maya's illusions seemed real, only the mundane gross vibrations of earth. The glory, height and depth of Soul consciousness lay dormant in man, waiting for him to ignite the flame within the heart.

"That which man desires he will have," spoke the Master. "Yet it must be utter dedication to that which he seeks. God brings no mysteries to man. Man creates the mystery by his ignorance. Let him seek the Path of the Golden Dawn that he may know and sip from the Holy Grail, and sever the chains of karma. Let him know the stillness within of peace profound."

Now was seen the Path seeping through all the earth's travail, bringing the Light of the Rose to darkness. Through the maze of man's material and objective thinking and action a new dimension of cosmic quality was awakened in man. Humanity once more was headed back to his divine

94

heritage, oneness with his Creator. The Master Path directs and aids man to make the journey to the High Mountain of Illumination. Outside the Path man drifted on the sea of maya's illusions and duality. The Path beckons, but man heeds not, seemingly content to wallow in the quicksands of temporal gayety. The sterling quality of everlasting life, the exalted music of the spheres, the close rapport of the Masters, was lost to all but the dedicated disciple surrendering all to find the lost Word of the Logos. To these, the Path became the "Lost Horizon," the open road to Shangrila, the key to the Stone and the Elixir, the luminous trail to the Most High Mountain.

"As you know, Pensatia," continued H, "before one is admitted to the inner school of the White Brethren, one must tarry at the outer portal of the earthly Order. There all must pass the boot training and attain the basic foundation. One's outer self must be purified, negative karma liquidated, or transmuted to love and harmony. All must learn the primer of occult law and master the first esoteric steps to the Golden Dawn. When, and if attaining this first passport, the Master leads one to his inner initiation and meeting with the Guru. Thus, one by one, man starts the pilgrimage to the fabled Alchemy of the Rose. Through the crucibles 'he makes gold and gives gold.' Yet before this happens he must adjust to and master the twelve strata of consciousness."

How graphic did the Master H explain the start and finish of the esoteric Path. How patiently he pointed out the pitfalls, the pull of the left-hand Path. How clearly he revealed the way to the Cosmic Cathedral within man's heart, where one experienced peace profound and heard the Voice of the Silence. How comforting his words to every sincere student. Yes when the student is ready the Master appears.

95

How easily he, the Master, would attune one to the green of nature and the humanity of man. The disciple feels enfolded in his love, humor and mercy. After every sojourn in his presence, one resumed daily duties refreshed and fortified for the arduous climb to cosmic consciousness. Communion with the Master is electrifying and progressive. One is lifted in that profound peace of that stillness nested in the flame of one's heart.

At each victorious lesson learned, the "well done" of the Master echoes from Akasha down to the student. Even when sorrow, loss and trials of mundane living brought its toll to the human heart, one knew this would pass. Thus in detached understanding of Cosmic law, all experiences of the Way one faced with patience and joy. One weathered the rocky climb upward. Often, at the bend of the Path, the Master wafted their consciousness to the Cosmic Garden, and there one rested in the beauty of fourth dimensional nature. There, the Master would tarry and answer questions and show the student the way ahead. Then when transported back to earth vibrational level, the student became steadier and balanced with new strength. Each knew God and the Masters ever guided and protected them. Thus a tranquility blest their steps, and the AUM of the spheres poured its melody through all the harshness of their discipline and earth trials. They thanked God for the Path and the esoteric dimensions.

Often when life's vicissitudes looms dark, when the beasts within man seek to destroy the spiritual, when the Path seems to dim into the spurious illusions of maya, it is then the esoteric student of the Rose must tighten his cordelier and tramp patiently through the bogs of temporal chaos and, with faith, know the crucibles will pass. Always in the dark night of the soul is the Master and the Path.

Even though the student may not see, doubt not. Substantial it is and will be.

"World without end," spoke H, "the Path eludes one only as one loses faith. Keep firm, steadfast, never taking your feet off the passageway to the luminous Rose of Life. With every victorious step onward, the stronger becomes the awakening of the chakras, the closer the rapport with the Master.

"Rest, now, Pensatia. We will meet again," the Master concluded.

Obeying, I saw the Master depart. "Until another day," echoed his parting words.

❀ Chapter Three

AGAIN I meet the Master H walking the Path holding to his gnarled staff. Slowly he traveled the King's Highway, intent on the neophytes, those young on the Path, those bowed with the weight of their boot training. To these he paused, easing their first steps in the crucibles of alchemy. Though as yet they were not conscious of his closeness they did feel a sudden influx of faith. They caught a glimpse of the Cosmic afflatus to come, like singing birds of spring. The hope and promise of the Path shone like molten gold. Thus they bore onward and upward, dared all to find the pearl of great price.

The Master smiled as he walked on, knowing he had aided the neophyte a degree nearer discipleship. To those proud ones with worldly ego, those seeking wisdom for material gain, these, with one sweep of his hand with the Staff of Azùl, were eliminated from the fabled Path of the Stone and Elixir. These disgruntled ones were easy fodder for the Black Masters. Alas, if they only knew the mockery and bitter ashes of their false steps. In another incarnation, these weak ones will resume their journey esoteric. They will realize there are no short cuts. Only *one* aim brings one attainment of the Rose of the luminous Mountain of Light!

Travelling with the Master along the Path we came to a green oasis and did seat ourselves beneath a shady tree by a swift running stream.

"Here," spoke H, "let us rest and converse about aspects of this noble Path. Many students think of the Path as rugged and bound by iron-clad discipline. Yet as they traverse onward they find a fluidity, a loving tolerance, a sweet warmth, a lightness of spirit never found on the harsh road of objective materiality and illusive maya. They find vision, foresight, and that extra sensory perception. They experience the influx of the Golden Flame infusing all life. As one progresses, even bitter waters turn sweet. All ugliness is transmuted into a divine symphony of harmony and beauty. The heart's wisdom is revealed to the disciple. All toil and labor becomes exalted service for God, the Master and humanity. This Path is the 'bridge' all must cross to become Christed. It is the safe, sure road to divine consciousness. Upon it man quickens his genius and cosmic heritage to birth. It is the infinite alchemy transmuting the gross in man to divine level. The student starts in blackness and ends in the White Light of the Golden Dawn.

"The Path is man's supreme gift from the Creator. The Hierarchical Brethren in White guard the archives of the deeper esoteric mysteries, leading the neophyte and then the disciple softly through the initiations of earth, water, fire and air. On this journey winding through life's vicissitudes man cultivates and waters the Living Rose within himself and nurtures it into bloom from his own heart. The

Path leads to the purple mountains of the soul's Shangri-la. Ever the Path beckons, calling to man as he journeys through earth life. Always the Masters stand by, waiting for the ready student. For when the student is prepared the Master appears.

"The Path, a 'Rock of Gibraltar,' never swerves from its Cosmic mission to unite man with the Oversoul. In slumber or waking, even amid the 'Way of all Flesh' the Path shines through man's ignorance. Thus it is, man has every opportunity to avail himself of the King's Highway. It is his denial of the Path which creates man's destructive cause and effect.

"The Path speaks through great art, music, literature; through nature and universal contact with evolved personalities. Yet again and again, man drifts on the Sea of Maya and the duality of objective living which ever binds one to the exoteric path. There are those naturals who live and walk with God, often unlettered, living close to nature. These are the blessed ones who have lived a Godly life through many incarnations, spreading joy, love and mirth. They know the Path as God. These serve the Masters, unconsciously living in heaven while on earth. To these people life owes an everlasting debt of gratitude.

"The Path is not conspicuous to the masses, but flows in silence through man's earthly journey, hidden, until man's heart awakens and he walks through the open door to his spiritual illumination. As one progresses, and earns the right to go forward, one attains the usage of esoteric laws and Cosmic remedies for health, wealth and Soul Power.

"Come with me, Pensatia, to that inner alcove of healing," the Master beckoned.

Swiftly, with travelling cape of white, we came to Akasha's inner signature of healing and medicine. Here, as one lifts his consciousness to this altitude of dimension, one may partake and learn of the wonders of God's laws. It is a round-like tower of a room. Here a bearded venerable handed out the ingredients needed for one's health. As man and nations are prepared for these higher medicines they will be given to the world. Already many are being discovered by those pioneering doctors of the Aquarian Age. Here only the initiates and those able to sip of these Cosmic remedies can do so.

"Now, Pensatia, let this gray-bearded guardian give you what you need esoterically. Remember these herbal drinks contain all earthly elements, too."

Looking deep within my eyes for a moment, the venerable studied me. The Master H had departed. We were alone in this Cosmic laboratory and dispensary of healing elixirs. The air was vibrant with tonic value. I felt an influx of circulation, as if regenerative forces were flowing through me. Then it was the venerable spoke and handed me a small glass containing a green and golden liquid with a drop of crimson bubble in it.

"Drink this three times a day. It has the ingredients needed to bring life, balance and strength to your body and mind. As yet humans have not discovered the physical counterpart. This drink does not interfere with any earthly medicine. It only brings more rapid healing to one's aid. By taking this drink three times a day will gradually eliminate all in the body that ages and destroys the tissues and cells of man. It will bring back the pristine glory of health and long life. All disciples of the esoteric Rose in some life are able to lift their consciousness and quaff of this elixir of regeneration. It heals all indigestion and creates perfect elimination and makes surplus weight disappear. Always take it three times each day, either by sipping, or all at once. All tiredness vanishes. The mind quickens. Heart and other organs become new. No one not initiated may try these Cosmic drinks. When the student is ready he will know. Enter the Path and know. Now also, Pensatia, here is a small white berry growing in the Cosmic Highlands. It is the Cosmic tranquilizer and brings peaceful, healthy sleep. It is the natural gift of the Father. Some day its equivalent will be given to man. This small white berry is a part of the AUM and Living Word; it soothes and quiets the nerves and brings healthy slumber. Take one every night, Pensatia, and all your body will respond in glowing health."

Thanking him, I promised to return each day and evening and take the remedies needed. I beheld hundreds of vials of different ingredients, saw herbs, berries, leaves of all different kinds, never seen on earth. Each was labeled for healing all man's self-induced diseases.

"Yes," explained the Cosmic Druggist, "the Creator is most merciful. Even when man, in ignorance or willfully, seeks to destroy his earthly temple, by entering the Path and preparing for the Golden Flame, at the ripe moment these Cosmic remedies are his to use. Yet never seek them unless initiated, or directed by the Master. They are too potent for those who have not their chakras open, in a greater or lesser degree."

I proceeded to leave. Master H was again at my side.

"Come with me now to the Alcove of Supply — or ready money."

With ease we sped away. Quickly we found ourselves in an alcove with a high vault and with open shelves stacked with money, currency of every denomination, as well as silver and gold. The shelves appeared endless. What was surprising, there was a slide or funnel where bills and silver currency, and gold, flowed down to earth. Yet only those conscious of their spiritual bank or reservoir attained it.

The more of it that flowed to earth, the more there was upon the shelves.

Again a venerable bearded Brethren in White appeared. H departed, saying, "Pensatia, listen, learn and write."

I obeyed and listened in rapt attention as the Cosmic Caretaker spoke.

"When man learns to rely on the Source and reaches here in consciousness he has only to ask the Cosmic Guardian, and one's needs are supplied. Yet remember, the law is: Hurt not another with thy gold. Circulate it, share it in some manner, and aid man to enter the esoteric Path and find this sacred chamber of endless supply."

"If this be so," I asked, "why does not money come to publish the Master's works?"

"O ye of little faith! Look . . ." He pressed a round and golden button, and gold, shekels and bills, rushed like a mighty torrent down to the one chosen to receive.

"As you see and know, Pensatia, so will it be. Never doubt what H tells you. Remember, if he who serves with you has not that living faith also, the way is blocked. Thus it is I bring a living flame to awaken his faith and point the way. Now know, even as you reach up here, you may take ample means to supply your daily needs, and more. By coming here you take not from another, or receive from earthly means. In what earthly channel it comes is not for you to say. I already know your needs, your desires. Yet also I know you seek to share this knowledge by recording your journeys with the Master H. Now ask for what you will, it will be granted you."

I did obey. And in my hand was placed a bright new bill of the amount asked.

"Every day, Pensatia, reach here in consciousness. Ask and receive. . . .

102

"I now speak of the Defender because of his love and care for you. Even so will the Horn of Plenty flow to him and, in slumber, all the Cosmic remedies be given him. He will be protected. If he perseveres he will in consciousness walk in the Golden Flame, and partake of all the wonders of God's gift to man. . . .

"Remember this, Pensatia. Even as the brain has innumerable compartments, each a repository for certain wisdom, even so — as below, so above. On the esoteric Path, whose essence is in higher dimensions, so also are there alcoves in Akasha pertaining to every aspect of knowledge.

"Let us now make way to the Alcove of Heart Interests and Matings."

Again we advanced into Akasha, to the Cosmic altitude where one may attain the talisman of Love. To have thus, I was told, assures one of meeting their complement of soul affinity on earth as well as in heaven.

We came to a high tree-shaded bank where the waters of life flowed by a silver stream. Coming toward us was the Essene, Jesus, and another of the Hierarchal Masters. Came also the Master H who saluted us with the sign of the Rosy Cross and bade us drink from the stream. Thus as one we partook of the waters of life.

Now the Dove of the Holy Ghost flew above the Essene's head and a brilliant light lit up his aura. He blessed us and pointed ahead to a shrine on a green hill, then departed with his companion.

Within the shrine, temple bells chimed. Another venerable greeted us and bade we be seated. Now he, the bearded Master, spoke.

"What seek you here, Pensatia? Have you your credentials?"

Pausing, I turned to H. But he also had departed. After

pondering the question, I answered boldly, yet with humble mien.

"My credentials are: I journey thusly with my beloved Teacher, the Master H, to learn, to record for man that which I witness. Now I seek to learn how souls may find and know their Cosmic mate. Or is such a fallacy? If you doubt my sincerity and credentials then denounce me now."

"How did you find your way here?" the venerable asked.

"The Christus Himself showed me the way, and I did drink from the silver stream."

Now he made the sign of the Rose of the Golden Dawn and bade me enter the innermost portals of the shrine.

"Well done, Pensatia," and he bade me seat myself on cushions of azure blue, and a purple flower was placed upon my breast.

"Be still and listen."

In the distance, flute music resounded soft and clear. Nearer came the calling notes of melody. Love supreme filled my heart. My consciousness was lifted up.

Suddenly a rose flame blazed from the center of the shrine. Sternly the venerable spoke, aye, commanded.

"Pensatia, enter the Flame of Love! All who have learned to walk in the vibration of Gold may enter here. At some time on the esoteric journey, the disciple in the Rose Fire will be initiated in Love's secret of knowing one's earthly and heavenly mate. First, know, all must bathe in the Rose Flame before they see their true affinity. Also is revealed one's karmic mates, or those by cause and effect fated to play a part in one's earth journey.

"Now, Pensatia, step within the Flame and face the truth!"

Before leaving, the venerable handed me a gossamer white robe and bade I shed my other clothes. I obeyed, and with a prayer in my heart and flute music softly playing, I plunged into the swirling rose-pink Fire of Eros. Even as I felt the magnetic rays about and through me a stillness there was, a quiet effulgence of complement. I felt the presence of someone drawing near. Looking about, I saw a man . . . whom I had known in other lives. My heart knew this was the ultimate Love. No word was spoken.

I then called, trying to go to him in the Flame. Yet another face drew me back, revealing a meeting to come. Yet a third showed itself. And from afar echoed these words from my Beloved:

"These, Pensatia, you must meet, know and love before we wed. But meet and wed we will before this incarnation ends."

All vanished. I waited to see more. Nothing there was. I felt purified, knowing all was true. The Guardian of the Shrine bade me come out. Obeying, I put on my travelling clothes and stood before the venerable.

"Pensatia, that which you saw in the Flame was your Cosmic mate, which nothing of earth or heaven can keep from fulfillment. Also was shown several others of karmic links who will play an important part in your life. All who have had the Alchemical Marriage must at some moment on the Path arrive at this shrine and see their true mate."

Now he did hand me a tiny vial of rose-pink. It was like a transparent flame. It had a purple jewel for a stopper, which glistened like a thousand suns.

"Remove the stopper each day, and place a drop of the flame of rose upon thy tongue, saying, 'God of my heart, and Masters, liquidate all karmic debts I owe to man that I may join my Beloved. So mote it be.' Say this once each day as you sip a drop from this vial, which you must ever carry within your heart. By so doing you hasten the coming

105

forth of God's most holy law, that marriage made in the heavens."

I thanked the Venerable of the Shrine, and turned to leave.

Master H was at my side. He smiled, saying, "The first you met in your Alchemy Initiation, did you not?" I nodded. "Yes, even though all seems naught, and a veil keeps you apart, yet know, even as the Flame revealed, it will be. And know, the second is one who loves you. Soon you will hear. Even so, one from far across the sea is another who loves you, and will come also. These ties first must be met and all karma liquidated or transmuted, even as you are liquidating in love and service, your karma. Know also, ECB by bringing forth my books by Pensatia, even so will he be blessed. Even so another who lived in the days of Mary Magdalen will aid and love you both, and even she will serve the Christ and her Master. (You will know her as you grow). I take you here, Pensatia, and have you record this because all who take the esoteric way must travel to this shrine and see their Cosmic and karmic ties.

"So closes the third chapter of 'The Path.' Go back to earth environment. Another day we will continue this travelogue."

❀ Chapter Four

Now the Master H did take me to a green and wooded valley. The High Mountain loomed bright and luminous down to those who walked the valley road. Some caught the Cosmic flash to man. They sought and found this Path which flows through life and set their feet on its aged landmarks, and lo, esoteric bloom budded in the valley. The warm earth sun, the gentle rain, the breezes seemed to sing a song of joy as the neophyte walked the Path.

"Yes, Pensatia, all nature feels and senses the man who takes the climb to the Most High Mountain. That is why a holy Guru may walk softly among the wildest of beasts and come to no harm. Yes, the footsteps even of a sincere dedicated neophyte leaves its daily mark upon the Path. Such is the might of the rose glow from the Hierarchal Heart. Here in the mundane School of Earth the masses walk, and often stay in their state of inertia unless stirred otherwise. The challenge of the atomic age must be met by all mankind. Its fiery spirit conquered within man himself. Thus only will the peace of a golden age be ushered in and mankind know his God. As man enters the Temple of Isis within the heart and lays his fiery nature in dedicated love upon the fire of heaven, then will the atomic gift of God be a blessing to humanity."

Now the Master sat upon a fallen log deep in the valley wood. Twilight moved softly over the land and a hush of stillness prevailed.

"Pensatia, every person who enters the Path must do so in the loam of earth, every step must be pressed and weaved with the hand of nature pouring its magnetism upon the crucibles of man. The luminous initiation of the Path only comes through the Cross of Matter. Only by transmuting the lesser to the higher, thus merging the two as one, does the neophyte become the disciple. Here the singing winds, God's feathered birds of color, the variegated bloom of flower, ferns, the cool dew mist raining on the good earth, the far-off whistle of a train winding over a mountain bed, the intermingling of people in the cities, all are the crucibles, the melting pot where the Rose and Lotus come forth. Be-

107

hold, the Path is life itself. When the Creator spoke : 'Let There Be Light' — thus was the Path spawned out to man. That man has not as a whole been aware of this, is his shame not his glory.

"The Path, Pensatia, is the center within the Wheel of Life. There are many spokes, each spoke finely connected with the center. If there is a flaw in any spoke, the spoke must be repaired or made new. For only stability and strength can have access to the center.

"The center within one's heart is the Temple of Isis. There, in rapport with the thousand-petalled lotus within the head, one communes with his Creator and becomes endowed with cosmic consciousness. Thus are the deeper mysteries of life revealed to the disciple when he is ready — on this winding Path, which follows through the dross and ignorance of man . . . ever waiting for the turning point of humanity . . . softly compelling . . . ever calling. The Masters know, at some point of incarnation man must make the journey to Cosmic Initiation. Yes, infallible the Path is, the living essence of the Wisdom of the Ages."

Now the Master H took his staff and did walk away and the green and wooded valley had a luster never known before; for he, one of the Masters in White, had left his mark upon the land. I pondered upon all that had gone before. I realized the Path is a step by step consciousness to ever higher dimensions of living. It is an orderly procedure of the authentic mystery schools to prepare one for entrance into the Golden Dawn and White Lodge. It is the ascent through earth to the Shangri-la of the soul. It is the above brought into the below, and the below into the above. I found the Path to be the alpha and omega of man's pilgrimage to the Most High Mountain. It is man's way back to the Father.

108

Starting from Cosmic sources the Path wanders deep into the loam of earth. Thereon man walks protected and guided by the Hierarchal Masters. The Path, I reflected, is one highway which never changes. Bound by the infinite immutable laws, cradled in earth, water, fire and air, nurtured by the Holy Grail, it stands staunch and everlasting. As I pondered, the esoteric Path glowed like a silver star in my heart. It softened the oft-times harsh experiences of life's crucibles. It pointed straight upward to the Most High Mountain. It flowed the dew of the Rose through all the dark nights of the soul. The music of the spheres poured its cosmic melody over the long stretch to the illumined heart of man. It was solid, like the aged trees on the wind-swept mountain passes, which bend but never break. So the Pilgrims of the Rose stay ever on the Path working in the crucibles of divine alchemy. They toil and undergo the initiations of earth, water, fire and air and thus cross the Bridge of Vision to the fiery pass to the Most High Mountain of Light. Yes the Path of the Living Rose bore witness to the Songs of Solomon, to the Psalms of David, to the Star of Bethlehem, to the Resurrection from the Cross and the sipping of the Holy Grail.

Now, at the beginning and the end, reaching its climactic zenith at the illumination of man, the Path, to the ever faithful disciple was as an evergreen tree, giving strength and perseverance to the ofttime footsore pilgrim of the Rosae Crucis. One knew man's immortal quest was impacted in golden print by every victory of man. Thereon the tears, the pain, the ebony heaviness of the dark night of the soul, passed into the Golden Dawn of oneness with Ra, the Creator of all life.

After each sojourn with the Master, even when his absence appeared long — yes, when the tide was out there was always that soft under-current of love and radiance as though the Guru had just walked by or was watching or protecting in the shadows. There was always that warm glow in the heart. One knew God was, the Master was, and in the full Aquarian Age man would know Him.

"O men, women, seek not to escape the call of the Master, seek not to evade the open door of the age-old wisdom schools, ride not by when the opportunity turns the door to a new life. Behold the Rose, the Lotus, bring their fragrance to you. Enter the Aquarian Path that your steps may mingle with those of the immortals. Let not this incarnation pass, unawakened."

Even as the Master's words echoed out into the valley, the city and far countries, spoke He again softly within my heart.

"Beware, Pensatia, of setting foot on the by-trails, beware of settling in a rut and not pushing on. Beware of the fox fire, or the will-o'-the-wisp, that which allures one to seek 'fool's gold.' Yes, beware of the Black Art, that which glamours the purely mundane pleasures. Remember the Path. Build your foundation firmly so that nothing of earth can sweep you from your moorings, even when opposition and friction prevail and ignorance crucifies you and the crucibles ever seek to destroy your labors towards the realization of soul growth.

"On this Path the disciple stumbles often. Many times his lesser qualities rise up and would devour him. Again and again the sorrows and ignorance of earth weigh heavily upon his heart. He hears the Masters' call to humanity. (Alas, so few heed.) He would share the glory, the song of the Mountain Top. Yet the masses pass on.

"Yes, there are moments of great loneliness, moments of despair when the Path dims and one seems surrounded by the fog and mist of maya's illusions. Yet these inevitable disciplines, tests and karmic payment due, are lessened as one is obedient and in dedicated love serves God, the Master and humanity. Yes, journey's end brings one to the spiral leading to the Bridge of Vision and the narrow trail to fulfillment and the illumined heart.

"Obedience does not only mean adherence to the Cosmic rules and dimensions, but a warm, loving closeness with man and nature, a receptiveness to leaf, tree and stream and mountain, an entering into humanity's heart, and a living desire to ease the karmic cross of man. The Path not only means the ascent to heaven but also the Path through hell. It not only means knowing the angelic beings, but the meeting and mastery of demons. The Path starts as a river and flows steadily into the mighty mystery and wisdom of God's cosmic ocean. One learns on the esoteric Path to transmute all harsh notes to the immortal melody of the spheres. It is the road of quest and search, and the finding of the Holy Grail, and the pearl of great price at the ultimate victory. One is also to meet on common ground the illustrious life and those on Cosmic plane.

"The Path is the open sesame to the Aquarian Age of a bright tomorrow. Without this luminous trail created by the Living Word man would stay in his self-caused ignorance. The Creator, in the merciful love for His creation, like the Good Shepherd He is, brought to earth the golden Path of the Lotus and Rose and made possible for man, by his earned efforts, to discover the way back to the Father's House. This is the meaning of all sacred books and scrolls, past, present and future. All true Cosmic books speak in unity of the essence of the ancient esoteric Path to Cosmic Consciousness and the Illumined Heart.

"Yes, Pensatia, and all who read — the Path is. It ac-

111

cepts you or belches you into your self-caused ignorance. The Path is a precious gift to man, for him to unwrap himself. Man must open the gate, enter and walk step by step to the Shangri-la of the soul and body. As man sleeps unconscious upon his bed until he wakes to life of day, so man sleeps in his ignorance, unaware of the esoteric highway to the Most High Mountain.

"Now behold the man who is as a *sleeper* in life's arena. He is dilatory, apathetic and a cautious yes man, one who dares nothing or accomplishes anything save to please his physical senses. By catering only to the objective and material side of his being he slowly and surely commits suicide. He is sluggish in mind, and while his physical body may be vital with animal gusto, there is no vision or rapport with his spiritual self. Thus he is like a splendid animal. Yet often the animal reveals more unconscious adoration to the Creator than man.

"Now let's look at the man who ever seeks to find his center of contact with the Oversoul. He is alert, alive with purpose. That is, he realizes the Creator is. He is weary, and with a divine discontent he springs away from the orthodox, from the mass thinking. He reads and ponders on the great writings of the immortals. He appreciates art, the music of the masters and studies nature in all its beauty and contrast. He loves people and is kindly, yet has a healthy sense of humor. He ever seeks to know, to dare. He recognizes his lack and is ready to start as a neophyte and to weather the boot training and crucibles of the esoteric Path. Such is the difference between two persons."

Now day's end softened the evening shadows as the Master bade me return to earth sunset until break of day. So closes the fourth chapter of "The Path."

❀ Chapter Five

IT WAS NIGHT. Ebony blackness lay heavy upon the Earth land. Yet in the sky above a thousand stars shone down to man. Supersonic sounds broke through the peace of nature's rest. It was then the Master came. As of yore, he spoke within my heart, saying,

"Take thy pen, Pensatia, and write my words to man."

Thus I obey and record his message.

"The Path is like a mine. The gold is there, yet man must dig within his self to find the shining Light, the Living Rose, the thousand-petalled Lotus. The Path has its source in the temple of the heart, there in the white and crimson flame of Isis unveiled. Heaven's splendor is revealed to the initiate, the true disciple of the Rosae Crucis. The long journey through the outer portals culminates in that Most High Mountain of Cosmic heights. Thereon, the disciple, having crossed the Bridge of Vision, is home at last. Truly the Father greets him. Behold, the Hierarchal Masters greet him, and the royal purple is laid upon his garments. Attar of roses, the dew of the rose, is sprinkled upon him. The wand and alchemical staff is bestowed upon the faithful, weary traveler, and by his side is the Cosmic affinity of Souls. Yes, neophytes, postulants, disciples, the long arduous Path, the crucibles, the initiations, end in the glorious sunrise of Cosmic Illumination and oneness with all life.

"Every dimension of consciousness is man's at the summit. He has mastered each step of the Way. Weary yet undaunted he stands erect. In the afflatus of the Rose of Life he looks back and remembers with gratitude the long sojourn in the crucibles and the alchemy trail, the boot training, the raising of the kundalini to the thousand-petalled Lotus, that indescribable union with the Creator and the White Masters, the Brethren of the Hierarchal Hosts. He

113

remembers too that unforgettable first revealment of Cosmic Consciousness, and the awakening of nature within his heart. The exalted friendships on the 'Bridge of San Luis Rey.' He remembers love's touch in all the lowly tasks of service and mundane duties. He remembers with joy every step won on the way to the Most High Mountain. Yes, he remembers all and knows every experience along the way was holy ground.

"The Path," the Master spoke on, "is the Cosmic blueprint for man, the key to karmic liberation, the formula to man's awareness of his Creator. It is the link between Heaven and Earth — the esoteric school all must enter — and, in some incarnation, graduate into discipleship and mastership. Man finds the Path as he searches, as his heart yearns to find his God, as he dedicates his life to service and the awakening of the Alchemical Rose.

"At first, rarely, does the neophyte become aware of the actual Path. As a rule, only as one passes the grueling tests of boot training does one sense the first inkling of the real Path within one's self. Little by little the pilgrim to the High Mountain learns and masters the fundamentals of the outer initiations before he knows by first-hand experience the Path is and the Masters are. This effulgence of Light which comes to all sincere students of the ancient Path of Alchemy must be earned. It cannot be acquired or given. Man himself must walk the Path and bring to birth the Philosopher's Stone and Elixir. True, God's grace and mercy is ever at hand. But man must earn this Cosmic knowledge. Often many years pass before one wins the green harvest of the Golden Dawn. Yet come it will sooner or later. After the travail comes the regeneration, the resurrection of man. The outer and inner merge and become one in the Alchemical Marriage.

"The Path reveals the four dimensional signature of all life. It is the unveiling of all mysteries, the cohesion of the above and below. The Path is the jeweled diamond man must mine and cut himself and which at last shines out from man, proclaiming his spiritual union. This awareness does not come about at once, but takes patient toil and faith. One must take a step forward, no matter outer storms or stress. One must know the bluebird ever sings within one's heart. One must feel and know the glory born in each day upon the Path. In the dark night of the soul, when one seems deserted and alone — in that initiation which, if met — will bring one into the Golden Dawn. It is then one must by faith, prayer and service, know the darkness will pass and that in the shadows the beloved Master stands, protective and comforting. This is ever so when, where no supply is visible and all outer props are knocked out from under one. Rise up and declare that which you desire. And even as the flowers and birds of the air are cared for, even so will the Creator care for His human creation. Yes even though days may pass, yet the tide will turn and out of the darkness one will walk into the effulgence of the Golden Dawn. Remember this when the Dark Night falls upon you. When one does come out into the Golden Dawn it is as if a veil has been lifted, as if one can see and hear and feel in a new dimension of living. Every facet of nature, people, the everyday toil, is seen in their divine signature. Life, beauty, joy is observed everywhere, in the most commonplace objectivity a glowing radiance surrounds. Such is man's awakening when aware of Earth's Cosmic pattern and his spiritual destiny. Is this not worth working for? Is it not worth facing the alchemy of life — the grueling boot training? Yes, through the initiations of the mystic Rose man climbs and wins the Living Rose from the Cross of Matter.

"Through the many rounds of incarnations man refines his earthly temple, making it finally a fit temple for the Light. Man's heart is the shekina of the soul. There in its mystic flame man finds the stairway to the Most High Mountain. Man finds as he travels the mystic Path he walks hand in hand with God. He will become aware that the Masters are and that nature was meant to reflect God in all His glory. He will learn that universal brotherhood is Cosmic law. As he is obedient and refines his lesser self and perfects himself he becomes master of nature and learns to work with the Creator's plans. He becomes a conscious co-worker with the Cosmic Father and the Hierarchal Masters. Remember, on the Path you meet the ignorance, the negation of humanity head on. For every step forward, there are those who ever seek to tear you apart. For every victory, there is that pull backward until one overcomes the law of duality and rises in consciousness to the Most High Mountain of spiritual fire. This is inevitable, the pull and opposition of the climb to Cosmic Consciousness. Without this conflict man would not have the initiative to even search for the Path, let alone enter it. Yes the Creator, the Living Word of the Logos, has placed inevitable laws here. When man learns to work with them all is harmony, brotherhood and fulfillment. Nature expands and reflects the glory of God. Man has found the center within himself. From then on, in peace profound he works and serves God and the Master, thus he helps in the great work of lifting humanity a step forward in its soul evolution.

"The Path is no shifting sand but a Gibraltar of man-creating soul fibre in all human relationships, tearing apart maya's illusions, revealing to man cosmic consciousness. It is the purifying flame of love transmuting all the lesser into its divine signature. It is the divine essence of wisdom circulating through all the trials and travail of the way, awakening man to the reality of the Hierarchal Masters and the liberation from his mortal self. The Path is the Cosmic wayshower of the Aquarian Age, the direct formula to life everlasting and the regeneration of man. On it man walks the circular way, and prepares himself through obedience to Cosmic law and dedication to God.

"When the student is ready the Master appears and guides one to his earthly mission, and leads one softly through the lesser and major initiations, leading to fulfillment of illumination, earthly and heavenly. This is a slow, orderly process. God and the Masters watch each step taken by the student, aiding the journey in all ways possible, that are compatible with one's karma. No matter how long, days, months or years, know, if faithful, patient and obedient, one will reap the harvest of fulfillment, know regeneration and cosmic consciousness. Slowly and steadily the heart will open to Light, Life and Love and the Living Rose will come forth in its divine sweetness and purity of Cosmic glory and will illuminate man.

"The Path, my people of all races, leads the way to that peace profound within man himself which all men seek. It is a Path of Cosmic integrity, it draws all faiths to its portal. It adds to, yet takes nothing of value away from the student. Like the shining sun breaking through the clouds of earth so the Path shines through all the storms of outer vicissitudes. Like the Star of Bethlehem it heralds for man a new age of liberation and service to humanity.

"The Path starts the neophyte on the basic foundation of occult and esoteric law, and when the neophyte has learned and mastered the boot training, he travels onward, ever towards pilgrim's rest high on the lofty mount of the liberated Rose. One learns serenity, patience, tolerance,

117

courage and positive thinking. One learns the art of opening his chakras, learns to see with the 'inner eye,' to hear from the 'inner ear.' He learns and finds communion with all life. The understanding heart opens to the waters of life and he becomes a new man. Such is the venerable Path of the ancient and mystical Rosae Crucis. All the arts, sciences and wisdom of the ages has ever flowed through its sacred halls of learning. It has sired philosophers, avatars, poets, writers, and the great saints of history. It has ever been the door to wisdom, study and the Voice of the Silence. A rugged Path, yes, open to the sincere searching student who wants wisdom and knowledge of nature and God more than breath. If faithful and obedient all sorrow, loss and trials are transmuted into joy and understanding. You will grow strong in spiritual consciousness, as well as earthly. You will know, where before you doubted. You will learn the inner signature of all life. You will realize God's bounty and Earth's wonders. You will be a gardener cultivating the divine art of living. You will hear the song of life resounding through all activities. You will feel the many splendored love of the One and the All. You will know the mystery of death and the secret of life. The whole earth will become alive for you. Endowed with consciousness, nature will open her heart and reveal her many secrets. Every aspect of the grandeur of Earth and Heaven will open up. Like the lotus of the East, all will reflect adoration to the Creator.

"In the many alcoves along the mystic way the Master talks and counsels, teaches the student the lessons to be mastered at each degree of the journey. Thus as man opens his inner chakras he partakes of the higher dimensions and vibrational splendor of cosmic scenery and the many vistas of the cosmic signature of all things. One's consciousness is carried into the pristine essence of all that is. Yes, this esoteric journey quickens and ignites the inner man and reveals his true affinity and oneness with God and the Hierarchal Masters.

"There are moments truly, when one finds on the Path the lonely watch, the hour of trial — the fires of the crucibles truly test the fiber of man's soul. Yet ever it is so. Even as the highest Masters were tried, and won, even so must man at some point of his incarnational progress face the initiations of earth, air, fire and water, and win discipleship and mastership. Remember there is ever the sustaining protection of all the Masters who have trod the Path before. There is the watchful eye of the Creator and the Lords of Karma ever bearing out man-earned blessings of cause and effect. For every step attained on the upward climb to the esoteric Mount of God man finds inner and outer fulfillment. He experiences in relativity all degrees in the art of living. He knows by inner initiation the glory of nature and the vast scope of life everlasting. All the color and super dimensions of consciousness are man's as he travels the ancient Path of the Rosae Crucis. Yet even as the pioneers blazed and toiled to bring civilization to virgin lands, even so does man pioneer into the unknown citadel of the God within himself. Therein, through the stillness of his outer self, he communes with the Father, and attunes to the Hierarchal Brotherhood, and Earth also.

"Now, Pensatia," H said, turning his attention to me, "listen while I answer many questions about this Path of Paths."

With deep interest I did listen and record these questions and answers from the Master H.

Question: "Why the Path — is not life itself the Path?"

Answer: "True. Yet man in his self-made ignorance has

not discovered this. Only when his heart awakens will man realize he has been on the Path all the time and knew it not."

Question: "Why the agony and the ecstacy, if the Path is? Why does not the Creator, and the Masters make it easy for man?"

Answer: "Man himself makes it hard, not God. When man is attuned to Cosmic law and works with the Father, then he rejoices at the crucibles and boot training. The Earth is a schooling for man's consciousness. Nothing is easily won. Dig your ditches, rain will come."

Question: "Is not the 'way of all flesh' the predominant way of man?"

Answer: "Not so. The divine pull within man ever gravitates one sooner or later to seek the Path and the Master within himself. The 'way of all flesh' is never man's key to Shangri-la. Remember this, and become aware."

Question: "Is not love a myth and affinities false?"

Answer: "Love of man and woman is and will be to life everlasting. It is a cosmic flame igniting the soul and heart of each to the other. Without this attunement all is false. No matter the legal marriages, affinities cut all barriers of race, creed, age. Each must flow to the other, as inevitably as the rivers to the ocean. It will come to all in some life and when lesser karmas are payed off."

Question: "Should one stay with his legal ties when he meets 'She' who fulfills the all?"

Answer: "One must and will sever all to unite with his cosmic affinity. In law and order this must come to pass. The Lords of Karma will see to it if man doesn't. Only true love of soul and heart is sanctioned by God and the Masters. It is better to cut the threads than live a lie."

Question: "Is not man often blinded by infatuation, often mistaking it for the real?"

120

Answer: "Yes, only because the passions rule instead of heart and soul. If one would meditate and be still the soul would answer and man would know. Real love is stillness, peaceful, thriving only in the bond of the Eternal. Through all earthly vicissitudes it glows in its splendor. Nothing of earth can mar its glory of fulfillment. Even though married many times legally, this love can come and lift man or woman to the love everlasting. Only then can the earth ritual and marriage bless and sanction this inevitable union."

Question: "Why so many mismatings?"

Answer: "Because man is not prepared, or ready for this many splendored fulfillment. One has many karmic debts to liquidate. It is written in the Akashic Records: Only soul and heart attunements proclaim real love. Thus one must be evolved to claim his own and be liquidated from infatuation's lure and the enslavement of the passions. In real love, physical union represents a sacred fusion with the Creator. As above below, as below above. One's Cosmic and earthly love comes when the 'inner man' recognizes and knows."

Question: "Do the Masters ever tell the disciple falsely?"

Answer: "A real Master, *never*. What is told will be. Yet be sure you hear rightly and not your desires speaking. There is no time issue. When man is ready the 'gong' sounds, and that proclaimed by the Masters comes forth."

Question: "Is divorce right?"

Answer: "One is already divorced if love is not there. The law only legalized what is already. Yet be sure that love is not before the act is made lawful."

Question: "Are contraceptives and birth control pills sanctioned by God?"

Answer: "No. Only transmutation. Self-control or continence is Cosmic law. All passion is under control of the soul. Only pure love is master of birth control. To use other means degenerates man. Though these ways will be tried, yet will fail in the end."

Question: "Is it right for man and woman to live together unmarried?"

Answer: "No. Cosmic law states: One must be wed by God's law and man's also. There is a special grace for soul mates, when impossible circumstances keep them apart. Only then does God's blessing state in God's eyes they are eternally wed. Thus they dare and rightly so to live their life of splendor without the mundane rites. But this is exceptional. Such was the love of Mary Magdalen and the Essene, Jesus."

Question: "Why the ebb tides and the high tides of the Path? Why cannot the student find a short cut to illumination?"

Answer: "Because there is not one. A short cut is only 'fool's gold.' One must earn his way to the High Mountain. Every dimension of consciousness must be mastered. Only by slow and steady application can man rise to his lost glory. All who proclaim a short cut are charlatans and deceivers of man. Such are spawned by the Black Brothers of occult magic. Beware of such."

Question: "Why are so many students poor in worldly goods?"

Answer: "Because one must lose all to gain all. Yet these same students learn that God always provides for their needs. When they learn the laws and reach up to the source, the bounty of God flows rich supply to them. Have faith, learn, grow. Dig your ditches, rain will come. No man is ever poor if he is rich within."

Question: "Is all illness curable?"

Answer: "Yes, even when Doctors give up. God can heal

instantly if karma and grace permit, and man's faith prevails. Ask, believe, it will be."

Question: "Can man live beyond his allotted years, or must one succumb to 'three score and ten?'"

Answer: "Man's allotted time cosmically is 144 years. As man serves and becomes illumined and lives according to Cosmic laws he most assuredly lengthens his life span. The statement in the Bible refers to the unawakened man. Also the years were not meant to be taken literally. Cosmically they meant many more years than stated. Each cycle of age should mean soul growth and advanced wisdom and inner power. There are those advanced souls who finish their earthly mission sooner than others and are called to do greater service on higher dimensions, or a karmic debt cuts short their earth life. Yet this too can be liberated by prayer, meditation and service. Trust God and love greatly, live naturally, and God will bless you with long life. The Golden Flame is the Cosmic Healer and regenerater. Stand forth, obey and live."

Question: "Does one suffer in death?"

Answer: "No, death is kind. One may suffer before, but not at the passing. It is peaceful and beautiful."

Question: "Is regeneration possible? And can it be brought about by mundane means?"

Answer: "Regeneration is a Cosmic fact. Mundane means aid only. When the inner becomes regenerated then the two may work together. In the Cosmic, from the Guardian and dispenser of Cosmic medicines — herbs, drinks, etc. — every student or disciple ready can reach up and attain the many phials for regeneration. Earth means are but the shadow of great Cosmic discoveries, when man is ripe for them. These essences work like miracles, lifting man to true regeneration of body. So obey. Seek and you will find."

123

Question: "Will America fail in its destiny?"

Answer: "Never. Adversity, trial and the crucibles it has and must face. Yet it will survive all and blaze its spiritual destiny to all the world. False leaders will perish, and a man of the people will come forth as another 'Abe Lincoln.' "

Question: "Is the Aquarian Age now?"

Answer: "We have just entered its outskirts. We are indeed being ushered into an advanced cycle of splendor. Go with it O man and learn."

Question: "Is there life on other planets?"

Answer: "There is. Hesper or Venus is the most highly evolved planet. Man must first reach it in consciousness before it can be reached outwardly. Otherwise man could not sense or see the Venusians or their scenery. The vibrations are rare and of the highest. There Cosmic laws are known and practiced. There what we know on Earth is infantile to them. As man contacts the Path and passes the Bridge of Vision, then will he be able to see and converse with the Hesperians and others that Phylo spoke of in his 'A Dweller on Two Planets.' "

Question: "How long does it take for man to become illumined?"

Answer: "It depends on one's past incarnations, his karma; and above all of these — his application, dedication and the opening of his heart and how he passes his initiations — according to his seeking, obeying, serving and living the life. Not even the Master can say just when Cosmic Consciousness is. It can be accomplished in one life. Sometimes it takes several lives. One does not measure the Path by time. Seeking God and the Master and wisdom of the heart more than breath can bring early illumination. Slowly and steadily, by application and obedience man is liberated from the duality of maya and knows the oneness of life."

124

Question: "Does illumination come to all alike?"

Answer: "The end obtained is the same. Yet there might be a difference relatively in the awakening. To some the cleavage of the centers are more drastic than others. (Read 'The Flame of White' in 'The Master H'). Yet in all illumination there is the same unity of pattern, the same sensing of the Light, the same consciousness of higher dimensions. Read Jacob Boehme, also Swedenborg."

Question: "Does the Path open its portal to all people?"

Answer: "Yes. Yet only the sincere and dedicated make the grade. The others walk out, back into the veil of maya and their self-made ignorance. Man himself cuts his tie with the Infinite. Only he himself can open the gate again."

Now the Master assumed his travelling cape of white and walked away through the golden haze of the Path.

"The fifth chapter of 'The Path' is finished, Pensatia," came his words. "Rest for a day, a night. Then arise in the early hours of the day and meet me with your pen — and thus record the sixth chapter of this journey esoteric."

A soft fragrance of attar of roses, like incense rare trailed after him. I realize to write of the Path one must truly observe, listen and heed that which the Master relays.

So, obeying, I will relax and partake of nature and earth activities, coming back refreshed, ready to go on with my assignment into higher dimensions.

❀ Chapter Six

HIGH UP in the hierarchal retreat of the mountain of the White Brotherhood Master H called and bade me welcome. There on a rustic porch overlooking a green valley, with wild roses climbing over the bannisters, we sat, and the Master spoke:

"Pensatia, here we will continue our talks on the very, to some, mysterious Path leading to the open Book of Life. First, Pensatia, sip from this delicate glass goblet containing the Wine of Life."

I obeyed. It sparkled in silvery and golden hues with a tinge of bubbling crimson drops like dew of the rose. I sipped, and new life, new joy and peace flowed through my being.

"Such is the Path, Pensatia. It contains all the ingredients of light, life and love. As the student embarks and bears the crucibles, the boot training, the initiations when ripe, all the life-giving drinks cosmically and earthly are given him. The circular flow and vibrational opening of man's inner chakras attune him to all the archives of wisdom. The great profound secrets of nature, space and inventions-to-come are there in Akasha for man to bring to earth, when he is ready.

"Here, as we sit and talk on this esoteric citadel, as we breathe in the air of the Gods and the Masters, we are partaking of that which all men may do, when ready and purified through initiation. Yes, the Path winds upward here where one may tarry and sup with the Master. Anytime, anywhere, the Master will some time call and one will journey here in conscious rapport with the Guru. So heed the rugged steps of the Way. Remember to bless each step, each cross that is yours to bear. It will pass and your wounds will heal, your sorrows turn to joy. Health such as you have never known before will be yours, for as your self-made karma and ignorance turns to wisdom and obedience, the Rose of Life will start to bloom from your heart and you will realize the Path is within man himself, which all humanity must eventually find and walk. This is the only Path

126

leading to life everlasting. This is the 'Mecca' all religions have at their center, which few know about. When man finds this 'center' then all will worship at the 'inner' cathedral, of which Christ and all the Avatars spoke.

"In this Aquarian Age man will and must find the Bridge leading to consciousness of the oneness of Earth and Heaven. He will learn to synthesize all life and speak a common tongue with nature and all mankind. Those not advancing into the esoteric heart and wisdom of this age *will not, can not* survive, for the Light of Aquarius will be too strong for them to live."

The Master paused. He pointed far down into the green valley below the veranda. "Look, Pensatia. See the beams of Light flowing downward. Watch as it touches those who walk the valley roads. With each ray of light wafted from higher dimensions man and nature are ignited, consciously or otherwise. According to their status quo of evolution, a quickening always follows this flowing of light downward from the Masters' abode. Thus it is the Creator ever flows the Word to man, knowing all races must find the way to that Light within man himself, that kingdom of which all the Avatars have spoken."

It was most scintillating as I gazed far down. The wonder, the profound love of the Creator for His creation warmed my heart with reverence for God and the Masters — they who through trial and the fiery initiations have won and stand in the vanguard of this Aquarian cycle.

How little the layman knows of the grandeur, the depth of the Path, the Cosmic discoveries, the gradual attainment of the Light of the Illumined Heart. How little man realizes the sacred privilege of walking the Path. How sublime — the agony, the ecstacy. Little do they realize the joy of victory over maya and the peace which comes with the meeting with the Master. So be obedient and, you who seek and find the Path, brave the boot training, build your foundation, know you will reach the Most High Mountain of the Living Rose within your heart. Until humans know the Path, they are indeed earth-bound, and are ignorant of the reality and the celestial heritage of their inner centers of attunement with the Masters and the God within. The Voice of the Silence has no meaning for them. They only live in a worldly dimension, believe only in objective experience and put reason and logic above every thing. Blinded they are to the coordination of the above and the below. The melody of the spheres, the communion with nature and the Masters are to them a myth, a child's fairy tale. Stagnating, self-centered, wrapped in the tinsel and "fool's gold" of maya, they commit slow suicide. To live wholly and vitally man must cultivate the Cosmic pattern of his life. Soul awakening must be. When this is, man becomes the true disciple of the Living Rose and the Masters. Akashic records are his to read. He is at home in all dimensions. This is the goal, the beacon of all humanity. It is the melting pot of man's unity with God. It is the only way of peace within and peace without.

"Yes, Pensatia, right in the midst of your everyday life shines the road of liberation. The answer to life's meaning, the great adventure of light and life everlasting. It is the one-pointed trail to the Most High Mountain of Cosmic Consciousness and alchemy mundane and esoteric. Right in the midst of life is paradise. In man himself is the Garden of Eden. The Rose of Life grows from the garden of the heart as man cultivates it. It blooms therefrom and liberates man from the Cross of Matter."

Now, high in the Masters' retreat, H did bring out a violin. He played, and all the haunting sadness, the exalta-

128

tion of love, all the merry sweetness, the folly-play of the winds, the mystery secrets of the deep, the Voice of the Silence, the surge and vitality of life — all notes resounded from the Master's touch upon the violin.

He paused. "Thus must man learn to make music from all experiences of life."

Now he brought forth a canvas, and lo, all aspects of Earth his brush painted in color and life splendor. The ugly, the beautiful, and the raw of nature and man stood revealed in their Cosmic origin and divinity. One gazed in meditative reverence and awe at the Cosmic splendor and message of the Master's work.

"Such," spoke H, "is the goal of every true artist. All who wield the brush and the canvas must ever anoint their creations with the Fire of Heaven and the Dew of the Rose and impart their colors from the archives of the Masters and the secret mixtures of Hermes. Thus will their work be immortal and last through aeons of ages. Thus you who write, paint or seek the arts, rise and walk the Path of the Alchemist and brave the initiations of earth, water, fire and air that thou truly represent the genius of your soul and serve God and the Masters through the arts.

"Down through the ages, the Avatars, the Masters, those from all races and walks of life have walked this esoteric Path of the Sages. Even in the Stone Age its pristine glow from heaven reached down to ignite the evolution of man. Yes, in the alpha and omega of creation God the Father declared the esoteric Path for man. In the Garden of Eden man and woman knew the Path and *lived* in the glory of celestial Light. Yet soul evolution made imperative that humanity learn through the School of Earth by self-effort the way of the Cosmic mandates. So tempted by maya's illusions, and the opposite of the Garden, man banished himself from Paradise to learn through friction, and choosing himself the way back to his Edenic consciousness. Thus only would he cease being a puppet and innocent of the objective world. Hence man through evolution and entering the Path must learn first-hand the Way to the Most High Mountain of Illumination and Cosmic Consciousness.

"Thus as flowers bud and bloom and give their fragrance out to Earth, as nature becomes lush with color and growth, as the stars and moon make brilliant the night sky, and rivers and mountains declare the glory of God, so man, by walking the Path, learns and reveals the oneness with the Creator and all life. There on the esoteric Path of the Living Rose the neophyte prepares for the meeting with the Master. Always, when the student is ready the Master appears.

"In the crucibles, through the Cross of Matter, through the alchemical laboratory within the heart, man masters step by step of the Path and finally wins the illumined mount of Cosmic Initiation. Self-made is the rugged neophyte who chooses to walk the mystic way. It takes guts, courage, obedience, a dedicated heart. First, one must eliminate all that bars him from building the foundation. He must transcend and transmute his weakness, his faults, and seek only the Holy Grail. Thus only can he bring forth the Rose of Life, that for which the Rose stands and all the authentic mystery schools.

"Some laymen on the outskirts, insist the Path is simply a figure of speech. Something intangible, of non-objective essence, an illusion of the senses. They claim the only Paths are those rooted in earth loam and plainly observable by man. Such is the blindness of men who walk the earth with their chakras closed, only the half of them awake. Steeped in materiality, they try to prove all things through their objective brain, not realizing the mind has access to higher dimensions of learning and the Oversoul. Grounded on earth, they themselves clip their wings and never realize heaven and earth are one. Like set stone, ignorant man stupefies his way to the Path esoteric. Thus unconscious of the Aquarian gateway he creates the closed door to fulfillment on all points of the triangle — the symbol of perfect self-expression."

Surely, I thought, as the Master paused, the Creator knows, the All-Seeing Eye, the Hierarchical Conclave watches the turmoil and usage of atomic power. Thus far and no farther, declares the fiat of the Word. Unless man and science work with Cosmic law, and cease their warfare, self-destruction is inevitable. Only the intervening hand of God can save His creation. Let us pray that this be so and that the mercy of the Creator save us from our own fate.

"Now even as life, the Path has its valleys, mountains, rough sea, its wilderness and barren stretches. Yet remember, if obedient and dedicated one passes safely through 'Dante's Hell' to 'Paradise Lost,' to the purple Shangri-la. Yes, the Path stands clear and shining in the midst of life, beckoning unregenerated humanity to enter its ancient gate and journey on to the Most High Mountain."

Now the Master did come close and led me to a narrow by-trail winding upward into the cosmic mist. I had my travelling cape of white about me, the Master also. With swiftness of light we bore upward.

"Where are we going?" I asked.

"Be patient, Pensatia. We are going to visit the Guardian, and bestower of man's innermost desires."

We now came to a circular golden dome-like building set in a beautiful garden of fountains and stately trees, green grass and sparkling colored flowers of all hues. Birds of vivid plumage sang with the music of the spheres.

131

As the Master and I went within the building a venerable Sage and Master greeted us and bade us follow him up a spiral staircase of pure gold. And above, the great Eye of Shiva looked down upon us as though reading our every thought. At the top the venerable bade me stand before him. Master H had departed.

Brilliant rays from the Eye bore into me. I knew all my thoughts, desires, stood revealed before the mighty Eye of the Hidden One. This was the ultimate censor. The verdict rendered here under the Infinite Gaze, was as cold steel, cutting my innards with steady survey. The venerable Guardian spoke:

"Dare you, Pensatia, say before the All-Seeing Eye that one or any of your desires are worthy to bring forth? Are they pure from your heart's altar, or merely of the flesh and of mundane essence? Know you not, only that conceived in the heart's fire, that sacred flame in the center of the heart, can objectify in life? All other desires are spurious and can not live, for it is the Black Art which spawns them. They die in their own materialism. Speak up, Pensatia."

Indeed I pondered deeply upon his words.

Earthly desires, though often wrong, are our karmic teachers. Through loss, opposition and wrong moves, we learn, we grow, often we pay in "Dante's Hell." Yet ever searching, learning upon the Path of Isis Unveiled, we reach up in humility and sincerely renounce all, even our most cherished wish of the heart, understanding the great Eye knows and will grant even the disciple's desire, born in the crucibles of the heart.

"Yes, Guardian, my desire which the Eye of Shiva reads, is worthy to be. Hence I ask, knowing the Father has even now granted such."

A golden glow poured down through the dome and bore

132

into my heart. I felt lifted up. Transcendent joy and a gentle, still peace, a fulfillment infused my heart. I knew for a certainty my bold and truthful answer bore fruit. I bowed my head in gratitude.

"Yes, Pensatia," spoke again the One in White as I rose to depart, for H was standing by, "if you had not the courage to speak up and answer as you did, that which you desire would never be. But honesty and frankness always is cosmically rewarded. May all students dare thusly when under the searchlight of the Cosmic Eye. Go with Master H, Pensatia. Thy desire is granted. Even now it draws nigh, ere winter flows into spring, it will be. Even so, students of the Living Rose, seek the High Mountain. Desire, speak up, have faith; face the Great Eye, fear not, that which is pure in heart will be."

"Come, Pensatia," bade the Master H. "We travel on."

"Where now, Master?" I questioned.

"On the Path," said H, "above and below, there is that barren spot where it seems there is no light, no joy, no anything. Even the Master, and the Path, is obliterated. The student walks through this dark night with only his faith to sustain him. Will he keep vigil through this barren test? That is the challenge of ultimate import."

Even as he talked we came to a gray twilight, a still, no man's land. A cold chill crept over me. I turned to the Master H for comfort. He was not there.

I pondered, for now all the long saga of my pilgrimage suddenly seemed futile. A despair pulled me into the depths of darkness and aloneness. No communication of any kind existed, just emptiness. Yet, there was something: a warm glow in my heart and a faith that this would pass and that in the shadows the Master watched.

I remembered this identical spot. Had not I and many

133

passed this hour of trial, this dark lane in the long journey upward? Yes, surely this repetition would not flay me. So lifting my consciousness to the Most High Mountain, I stood still and centered my feeling within the heart's flame. There in the very darkness, the cold austere grayness was as a benediction. It was as if the bluebirds of Shangri-la sang through the gloomy atmosphere, as if soon the Golden Dawn would break through.

It was then I heard the Master's voice speaking at my side.

"Pensatia, it is true. Always, at intervals, one passes over and again through the ebony agony of soul growth, the testing of the disciple. As one faces this moment, or hour, or days of the dark night of the soul, greater will be the emerging into the Golden Dawn, heralded down through the ages as the *splendor* of the esoteric journey."

Even as H spoke, that sweet scent of attar of roses filled the air. White light flowed down upon us. The Path ahead shone like old gold.

"Thus does one walk the Path," said the Master. "Out of darkness of ignorance into the wisdom of the liberated man. Yes, always one must pass through this dark vale and win through to the Bridge of Vision. Seek not to evade, or run from it. For in another incarnation it will be much darker and take longer to 'come ye out.' "

So closes the sixth chapter of "The Path."

❀ Chapter Seven

"Pensatia," spoke H, the Master, resuming our talk as we journeyed through the Path in review. "After the darkness comes the light. Even as stars come out and lighten the night sky, so the Master gladdens the heart of the disciple of the Rose. Thus one finds the Golden Dawn of Cosmic Consciousness surging through one's whole being. The whole wide world takes on a new dimension of beauty. One sees, hears, feels as if once again, and truly so, they saw all in its infinite design. Such is the purging, cleansing and opening of the chakras under the initiation of the dark night of the soul. Thus is Cosmic Alchemy the transformer of all that is gross and elemental.

"The Path, Pensatia, is a catalyst changing all earth vibrations into the wholeness of the divine pattern. Only by entering the esoteric Path does man find and know first-hand, nature, God and man. It is the Path of all the Avatars. The Way to the sacred citadel of the Living Rose. On it are all waters of life. Fire, earth, air and water must be met and conquered. Every beast of the wild within man must be tamed, and made to serve man's divinity.

"The Path glows through life's labyrinth, ever beckoning man to follow and tread the Way of the Masters. It never compels, yet its portals are ever opened to the sincere of heart. The Black Brethren dare not set foot on this hallowed Path. As man walks it, the Fire of Heaven, the Holy Grail, is given to the faithful disciple at the Mountain Top of Illumination. It takes a steady gait, a sober obedience, a courageous attitude, a humble sincerity, and utter surrender to the finding of the Wisdom of the Sages. When man becomes aware that there is a Path, the experience is never forgotten, for so plainly is the neophyte shown the reality of the Path. It is ingrained forever in one's consciousness. Like a luminous lighthouse it beckons man onward and upward to the Celestial Host. Until one becomes aware of this Path, he is only at the outer portal. It is the Cosmic mandate when entering the outer portal: Before one pierces the veil of Akasha and mounts the Mountain of the Gods, he must experience the Path. Otherwise he may belong in name to the esoteric school, but may never reach the inner temple of the Golden Dawn.

"Until one is vitally aware and initiated, one has no inner realization — only intellectual. The real Path rises unseen, unfelt save by the dedicated disciple, out of the outer, and from the inner consciousness of man. The heart is the door. Therein the pink-red flame of love generates up to the thousand-petalled lotus in the head, where the veil of light is pierced, and one stands in the presence of the Cosmic Initiator, the Christus. The 'Stone of the Sepulcher' rolls away and one is born into his Body of Light. The sacred chakras open and one drinks of the waters of life everlasting. One is crowned servant of God and humanity. Infinite power is his to command. All nature serves the disciple of the resurrected Rose. For love only rules him. His heart's flame flows to all life, for he knows he is a part of the whole. Such is the glorious harvest of the Path. Such is the victory of mastery within.

"The Path is a Cosmic university of infinite wisdom. In its halls of learning come the Hierarchal Masters, teaching and guiding the neophyte to the Holy Grail and the Rose of Life. From the first outer step the neophyte has the promise, if faithful and obedient to the boot training, the door of the heart will open, and one will enter the wisdom archives of the White Lodge and the Dew of the Rose will baptize one into the initiation of the Most High Mountain of Light.

"Little by little the student is infused with this glow from within. Slowly and steadily the chakras open and revolve to the infinity of God. By obedience, faith and application to the mandamus, one evolves and realizes his divine plan,

136

conceived and brought forth by the Word, that which created all. All along the Path, the student of the Rose and Lotus is tested, tried and given work to awaken his sleeping potentialities. If faithful, the promise of the Path brings victory and liberation to man and green harvest. Behold, Pensatia, the power of the Word flowing down to man. When aware and working with the creative mandates of God, the power is yours and all to use at will for the good of humanity.

"Every attribute and one's potential genius flowers under the tutelage of this ancient esoteric Path of the Rose and Lotus. It is a Path of sublimity, of golden light, of white magic, of humanity walking with God, of nature pouring out its secret wisdom to the disciple of the Rose. It is a Path of inner expansion into all strata of dimension, a Path of guidance of the Masters, a communion with the God of one's heart. It is a Path which lifts one out of the blackness of ignorance into the way of the living Rose of Life. On this Path walk the White Brethren and the Wayshowers of the Golden Dawn. Those men who exemplified and taught the ancient mystical Rosae Crucis. Those men who were humanity at its highest level and beyond into Cosmic Illumination. The illustrious Bacon, Boehme, Alden of the Rose and Golden Dawn, Pythagoras, Nostradamus, Madam Blavatsky, and numerous more.

"On this Path are the landmarks of those noble men who sacrificed and gave their all that man find the opportunity to fulfill his Cosmic destiny. Its price is not mundane but the dedication and obedience of man to the ancient archives of esoteric wisdom of the ages. A humble and sincere heart always finds entrance to this Path of Paths. It is the only key that opens the gate to fulfillment.

"The Path is that road man must take, sometime, somewhere on his earthly journey. All the Masters have walked it. Also must man. It stands in the center of life, in man himself. None can forever evade it, or escape its tutelage. There in its immortal mission it shines out to humanity like a lighthouse, ever beckoning one to the eternal Shangri-la of the soul; immaculate, immutable, infallible its mandates, yet fluid and flexible; the Path embraces all facets of one's pilgrimage through earth's loam, at the same time winding ever upward to the esoteric mountain of God.

"The Path is not a faint trail, smooth travelling minus of rough places. It is not geared to only summer weather or soft winds. Rather, at times storms and beasts of the wild prey upon it, seeking to devour or to toss back the neophyte or postulant or disciple of the Rose into the outer duality of maya. Only the allegiance to the Christus of the Holy Grail; only one's faith will carry one through the crucibles of the Path. Thereon man must weave the golden Robe of the Master. There he must make gold and give gold. All the lesser falseness of his earthly self must be transmuted to the divine purpose. Without this Path — the way back to God, the Living Word — man is at the mercy of the ever-drifting tide of maya, ever a slave to the illusions of the passing temporal. The Path reveals the divine signature and creative laws of the Cosmic. The venerable Hierarchal Masters walk and teach upon it. The Essene, Jesus, the Christed One, with all the wayshowers of past ages, are the vanguard, revealing to those who seek the wisdom of the Rose and Lotus.

"Like a fresh flowing river, the eternal hum of the AUM pours out its melody. The white dove of the Holy Ghost flies high in the vibrational heights ever ready to anoint the prepared disciple. 'Well done, good and faithful students of the Rose,' ever speaks out the Master to those who have braved the crucibles and won. Tenderly, with compassion and love, all wounds, sorrows and loss are retrieved and transmuted into peace profound. Death turns to life everlasting. No grave can hold liberated man who has the Rose of Life upon his heart. Such is the simplicity and magnitude of the esoteric Path for man. Day by day, life after life, pilgrims of the Golden Dawn and the Rosae Crucis start this glorious journey to the High Mountain, of which you, Pensatia, have written. Many turn back. But the steady, sincere, brave the winds, the storms, the boot training, and make their way up to the mount of Cosmic Consciousness. They study and work in the crucibles ever seeking the Elixir and the Philosopher's Stone. They are the alchemists, transmuting all to the pure gold of mastership. They are the ones who walk with God and nature. They are the ones who are lifting the Aquarian Gate open to man. They are the pioneers of the New Age, exemplifying Cosmic Light out to the ignorant.

"So let this Path, O readers, seekers, searchers, become your Path. Let it enfold you in its wisdom, in its peace profound. Let it quicken all that is dead in you to life and fulfillment of expression. Let it reveal the inner man to you and the glorious awakening of your heart and the meeting with the Master. Let the hand of the Father lift you to the waters of life everlasting and light and love. Forsake all lesser things, drink only from its fount, share and give out in acts and deeds all that you receive, lift in some way the veil of ignorance from the unawakened. Exemplify the fire of the Heart, the mystery of the Lotus, shower the Dew of the Rose upon the earth that Cosmic bloom spring up. Let your faith water all you contact, that a new inspiration be ignited in man, that he start on the Rose Path and know communion with God and the Masters. Let him learn to pluck the Rose of Life from the Hidden One and bring it forth from his heart. Let him cease the turmoil, anguish and escapism of maya's tyranny. Come ye out to the ever green vistas and blue and golden horizon of the citadel of cosmic consciousness and the Illuminati of the Most High Mountain. Fear not the rough passage. One will survive all storms into the quiet and peace of the Holy Grail and the initiation at journey's end.

"Such is the Cosmic mandate for all races of men. Such is the everlasting Word etched in Akasha. Such is the call of all the Masters visible and invisible. Like a sunset of manifold colors, or the pink radiance of sunrise, or the flowering of earth in all its manifestations, so humanity must and shall bring forth the bloom of the Rose upon his heart. The balance of the square within the circle must actuate every action of man if life is to survive and function in the Aquarian Age.

"Man's inner chakras must open and thus will he consciously drink from the Cup of the sacred Chalice of the Holy Grail. The Path is the reservoir of God's saving grace for man. It is the great Race man must enter to win and know life everlasting. It is the walk with God and the Masters all men must take. On it kings and peasants alike have traveled to the High Mountain. Along its trail battles have been fought and victory won. Hereon, the Essene, Jesus, prepared for his Cosmic mission. Here the philosophers and sages poured out their discoveries of wisdom for man. Here the sound of the AUM, the Music of the Spheres, the Elixir and the Stone, the Divine Alchemy of the crucibles await the pupil, the student of the art of making gold. Here one studies for the Cosmic University Hierarchal, the White Lodge of ancient lore. Here one, if obedient, proves within himself the ancient mysteries. As one attunes with the

Akashic Records one scans past, present and future, one realizes the law of reincarnation and bears witness to the hall of past lives. Here on the Path, one learns to liquidate past negative karma and create that which blesses. One becomes aware that he is a living soul in a physical body and that death can never touch his real Self. He finds the balance of earth and heaven and knows the bridge to unite the two. He finds the Path is he and he is the Path (a mystery revealed to the Initiate and the Disciple). The keys to the Kingdom are given to the student when ready.

"The Path is like a river, it ever winds to the infinite Sea. It is the only Path proclaimed by the Word. It is the Way, Truth and the Life taught by the Essene, Jesus, the Christed One. It is the immaculate print of life everlasting. For man to be aware of the Path and embrace its crucibles is to find the reality, the unveiling of the mysteries. It is to sit at the feet of the Masters and thus travel to mastership of oneself."

Now a crimson glow stole over the Path. A hush as of twilight mixed with the hum of the music of the spheres. Attar of rose and lotus scented the atmosphere. "Come, Pensatia, let us journey on."

We came to a great sea of vast expanse. Yet calm as a mirror, not a ripple on the silver glow. As we looked upon it a peace incomparable welled within us. Gazing deeply upon its mirrored surface one felt the Cosmic oneness with all life. All harshness, all not in harmony, seemed to melt in the tranquility of this sea.

"What does this mean?" I asked the Master H.

He answered: "Pensatia, when man learns stillness and walks and works from his heart center, he becomes calm as this sea before us. He is able to see in the depth and height of life. Through meditative stillness and mastery of his lesser self, he becomes conscious of this Cosmic sea. And as

Jesus stilled the storms of maya, so the disciple is able to walk upon the waters of life in calmness and clear sight, no matter the outer chaos. When the disciple attains this Sea of Calmness he is truly one with the Master, and henceforth is prepared to take the fiery and air initiations. Come, let us walk across the sea of water."

For a moment I hesitated. But quickly a sustaining faith was mine. I turned to speak with H. Lo, he had departed.

Again I was on my own. The water, though calm, was of seemingly endless dimensions, and so deep! Its surface was as silvery blackness. No one was present. Yet a rumble of sounds reverberated from the water's boundaries. It was as if all the savagery and wild beasts of earth sought to keep me from embarking on the tranquil sea.

I noticed every time my inner control slipped, a huge wild wave tossed upon this sea. So turning my thoughts away from the ever-changing turmoil of maya, I centered them serenely within my heart's temple, and walked upon the ocean of peace, and the great wave subsided.

A rainbow arched the waters. It was as if I floated over the sea, so light and easy was my walking. The more I advanced across it the more I was aware of the merging of all life with it. It was as if all nature and man became one with the Spirit of the Waters. As I pondered on this, the Master was again at my side.

"Yes, Pensatia, man becomes one with all the elements when he masters the elements within himself. Thus is the Path the teacher. Thus does the student of the Rose become victorious, and raises the kundalini to mastery in the thousand-petalled lotus. Now, as you see, in being able to walk this sea, which all must traverse, one comes into the green watered verdure of nature controlled. Henceforth even as the Masters, the disciple realizes.

142

"Next comes the fiery test. That which burns the dross, the negative accumulations of many lives, all which must be purged in the fiery furnace of the crucibles.

"Pensatia, let us close this seventh chapter. We will resume our journey in the next one."

Obeying, I did thusly.

✺ Chapter Eight

THE MASTER H now guided me over barren, rocky ground. All around was seen and felt the raging chaos of earthly life. Yet in the midst of this hustle and conflict glowed the golden Path of the Rose. It sustained itself by constant intercommunion with the Creator and Hierarchal Masters. Unnoticed by the ignorant masses, it vibrated in all its Cosmic glory, everlastingly the open portal to man's liberation from maya. Walking on the firm loam of the esoteric, we found wisdom, peace and strength to cope with Earth lessons.

Now, looking into Akasha's print we beheld a youth growing into manhood, destined to lead the world into the cycle of peace and brotherhood. One risen from the loam of the people, one though born afar, cradled by the eastern sun, yet wafted to the Land of the Eagle in boyhood, thus to prepare for his Cosmic role.

Yes, America will be rededicated by this man. Thus will the sunrises, the moon cycles, the seasons mature and proclaim this leader of the Aquarian Age. Behold the signs and watch.

The distinguishing feature of the Path was the feeling of the presence of God and the Masters. It was as if from the start one was on hallowed ground, marked by the footprints of all the Avatars, disciples and initiates who had attained the Rose of Life and the Philosopher's Stone. One felt here on this Path man would find the Kingdom of Heaven within himself. One felt, too, the crucibles, the challenge of the boot training, the discipline before passing the tests of discipleship and higher initiation. All this passes before the neophyte entering the outer gates to the Wisdom of the Ages. It gives one the realization of the depth and height of his pilgrimage.

At first the journey appears almost austere and forbidding. A great loneliness is apt to take hold of the beginner as he is tutored in a new dimension of thought and action. Yet also he feels, if sincere, the steadfast dedication to learn, dare and keep silent, and to lift his heart ever to the Most High Mountain on the Cosmic horizon. As esoteric joy and zeal ever stirs the student on the Path, he senses that through obedience and diligent toil in the crucibles, he will come out the true alchemist who turns all base matter into the pure essence of gold. Thus the looming hardships, the meeting and liberating of negative karma, the building of positive beautiful karma, the preparing for the Alchemical Marriage. All these degrees of initiation and areas of consciousness seemed only a blessed hand ever leading one upward to Cosmic fulfillment, so intimately does man and the Path become one and vice versa. One realizes by degrees the Path is the esoteric Cosmic pattern of man's divinity and earthly relation to nature. It is the divining rod which shows and develops man's inner attunement to higher dimensions.

"The Path," spoke H, "is the omnipresent voice of the Creator speaking to man. It is the golden flute call of the infinite to man. In all these various repetitions of explaining the Path, adding the sum total mandamus is man himself, the 'Columbus' who discovers the New Land. He himself must find and navigate the ship across the mundane Sea of Maya. His faith is the key to the finding of the Master; his obedience to the call of the esoteric Rose of Life. The Path is the road to fulfillment in all aspects of life. The Path is like a surgical operation, cutting out that which destroys man. It is like nature, healing the self-made wounds, transmuting the scars of cause and effect. It is the Cosmic scalpel letting out the impurity of man, bathing him in the waters of life. It is the great Physician saying, 'Come unto me all you who are heavy laden, and I will give you peace.'

"The Path is the kiss of the Prince of Peace awakening sleeping humanity to the Alchemical Marriage. All who enter the outer chambers are each pioneers seeking the Kingdom of Heaven within themselves. Yes, all the challenge of inner discovery is theirs. They, the alchemists of the Rose and Golden Dawn, work in their crucibles, ever seeking to transmute 'base' metals into gold. Those who realize — it is the inner gold of the Soul that is the true gold; those who do not realize this, fail as alchemists. The true alchemist can truly change the lesser to the higher, and the inner becomes outer, the outer inner. Thus is the gold of Heaven and Earth produced.

"Outside the Path man knows not his course or whither he is going. He drifts with the line of least resistance, or else he becomes a strict materialist. His only values are in obtaining 'fool's gold' and in objective seeing and building. The dimensions of the soul are void of one's realization. Thus it is man who bars himself from the 'Garden of Eden' by ever seeking to escape from the inner call of the Masters and the God of his heart. Outside the vale he wanders, with the keys to the kingdom within the silence of his own heart. There, in the sacred flame of that inner temple of the 'Rose

Dew,' man may attain oneness with the God of the Universe, discipleship with the White Masters of Hierarchical Conclave and attain the Philosopher's Stone and fabled Elixir.

"The Path is not that which you can walk on and off of without creating negative karma. Nothing is gained and much lost by so doing. Cosmic law states: 'When putting your hand to the plow, take it not off.' Slow and steady is the making of a neophyte into the disciple and Master. This process should not be interrupted but allowed to bud and blossom into the illumined man. Only by application, perseverance and walking ever upward does and will one attain the Most High Mountain.

"The Path has none of maya's illusions and changeability. It has no bribery or false turns. Glowing in its golden light, it leads straight to the High Mountain. In pristine essence of Cosmic law, under the All-Seeing Eye, the neophytes earn the right to know the Masters and pass the initiations to the White Lodge. Never think this can be accomplished in the outer schools. They only gave you the tools to enter the esoteric center of man, the heart's shekina."

Now, addressing me, H said, "As we travel along, understanding the over-all pattern of the Path . . . it is discernible to all who faithfully walk thereon. It is a vast blueprint of the way to the Shangri-la of man's journey through life. One realizes from the first solid step taken, the wisdom and wonder of the Creator's immutable laws. One, from the very first step upon this august Path, realizes the faint rustle of the Master's presence. He senses the law and order of the universe. He knows he has made the most important step of his life. Also that it is up to him to progress. One's application, zeal and absorbing dedication to the tutelage of the Mystic Way is the yardstick to Cosmic Consciousness and the finding of the Holy Grail, or the benediction of the Holy Ghost. One senses at the very start the profound altitude one must embrace to become the true disciple of the Rosy Cross and Golden Dawn. All realize, only as they earn grace and the guidance and communion with the Master, will such be. They know if they walk off the Path, it is their choice, and one which has great karmic ramifications. For weaklings, the Path is not. Only those who can take the harsh winds, the crucibles, the tests and trials of the Way, ever make their way to the Most High Mountain. Yet to those who stick, those who have faith and stamina, those who seek only to find the heaven and God within, those who renounce the lesser, the 'fool's gold' to find the All, these hardy neophytes God and the Masters aid, in all ways possible. All who start out weak, if sincere, may grow strong and often surpass those who are lacking in heart fiber. Such is the infallible mandate of the Esoteric Path: 'Give your all, or fall by the wayside.' The promise of the Path, one can depend on. All the grace of inner perception is awakened. The centers open and respond to all dimensions of scenery and thought. There is that internal glow of the overshadowing God of one's heart, that ever encourages one to climb on. There is that sacred aroma of attar of roses and the fresh dew of the fountain of life which ever renews and regenerates the postulant seeking the illuminated consciousness. *Above all else,*" H emphasized, "there is that profound peace which man gains as he walks the Path."

Now the Master H did waft me to the 'Isle of Samos,' that sacred grove of sojourn with the Master. There in that rarefied environment we sat on a grassy slope surrounded by the mystic Sea of Light, and rose dew rained softly upon us.

147

"Pensatia, on the Path, when ready, the disciple is transported here to recharge, regenerate and balance his earth and Cosmic attunement. It is only after much inner growth and outer service and obedience to one's progress, that one earns the right to visit on the 'Isle of Samos.' All the visible and invisible Masters of the White Lodge have rounded out their mastership here. Its green, soothing groves and scintillating Cosmic sparkle generates into the disciple's earthly body the needed alchemical harmony. This postgraduate course with the Master is needed by every disciple-to-be of the Path. One reflects and ponders on the esoteric chart of one's past, present and future. The Master points out weaknesses yet to overcome and reveals one's karmic harvest ahead. One familiarizes himself with seeing, hearing, feeling and acting on the higher planes and dimensions of thought. When the disciple leaves the 'Isle of Samos' rest assured, he is the finished disciple, ready to carry out his Cosmic mission, of greater or lesser degree. Here, too, before leaving, the Master bequeaths many earthly blessings. Often the bounty of Earth — love, money, health, travel, et cetera, are his in finding 'Samos.' All else is added.

"Yes, in the 'Isle of Samos' the initiate comes away the finished disciple, imbued in all the powers of the wisdom of the ages. Poised and ever working from the heart center — from that esoteric flame of light — he commands nature and bids all life serve him in the name of the Christus. He wields his Cosmic power to heal, bless, to make gold and give gold. Humble, dedicated, yet most human, he loves, for he has become love. He has wealth, for he is wealth. He engenders health to others, for he is health. His aura is positive, gold and purple, blue and clear-cut green, and most brilliant pink and white light covers him as a cape. He stands four-square in that circle of stillness, that holy silence of the heart's shekina, and behold, the Kingdom of Heaven he has found, and the Holy Ghost of the Sacred Grail. Such is the benediction of 'Samos' and the glory of the Rosy Cross.

"Come," spoke H softly, "let us go back to the Path. Close now the eighth portal of this travelog. May all journey towards 'Samos' who read these records."

I, Pensatia, laid aside my pen and did walk on earth's soil again.

❀ Chapter Nine

IT WAS the time of evening shadows falling. The sun was gently down, flowing softly through earth's atmosphere. It was then again came Master H. He spoke:

"Pensatia, let us sit beneath that stately tree and converse and learn what the Esoteric Path is."

"Yes, I answered, "thus in listening, will I record."

"First, realize the Path is no fairy tale, no fiction of man's imagination. It is a sure and steady road, clearcut, straight at times, winding at others, marking the way to man's peace and happiness and the awakening of mind and heart. It is the only road four-square which leads to paradise. It starts in the center of one's being and builds outward to the world. It starts in hell and rises upward to the stars. It grips man and holds him in a vice until he grows, learns and expands into cosmic consciousness. Yet it ever leaves the student free to choose, free to leave, free to act. As one does thusly, so changes his life for better or worse. The Path, my student of the Rose, is the one reality man can depend on in the midst of maya's illusions. None can escape it. In some incarnation man must start walking its ancient landmarks. Man must acquaint himself with the archives of wisdom and tarry in the many alcoves of its dimensions. It is not a road for sleeping, or easy walking. Not a road sired in the shallow hands of make-believe, or hollow fantasies. It is a hard and rugged Path of esoteric truth. Its materials are lasting, created from Cosmic loam. All who tramp its ramparts to the Most High Mountain of initiation must have stamina, fortitude, patience and the zeal to walk it at any cost. They must follow through even as the disciples of old and the venerable Masters, who sought only the Stone and the Elixir, and the White Magic of the Soul.

"Think not O egotistical man this Path is not. Think not you are the cock of the universe or that you are the miracle man of the ages. Not so. Only God, the Masters and the Path are the keepers of the Secret of the Ages. Only the golden disk behind the earth sun can reveal to man God's infinite design for man. Those who stagnate in their ignorance and earth ego will pass by the Path, and hence into oblivion. Those who claim only purely objective consciousness will be pushed into the reality of other worlds and the proof of man's soul. Those who are not ready for such, having played out and wasted their lives, the glory of Wisdom they have not earned. Thus many will pass out of life and await rebirth. Yet a few will turn and, in humble seeking, will enter the Path. These, God and the Masters will aid and show the Way. Thus does God give to all the opportunity to attain the Living Rose.

"When one enters the Outer Gate, one strips himself of all acquired thinking and starts anew, as a seedling. Little by little he grows and expands in consciousness, until the Living Rose of the Golden Dawn comes forth. This is no idle promise of the Masters but a positive attainment of the faithful student. As one progresses and is aware of Cosmic law and the ancient wisdom he finds at onement and green harvest at all points of the triangle. Every step taken and mastered brings man nearer to the Most High Mountain. It is a conscious self-revealing Path, giving man access to all dimensions of thought and action. Clear, direct are the mandates. To obey and practice the laws brings peace and fulfillment to man.

"One cannot repeat too often the salient points of the magnificent role the Path plays in the evolution of man. So never think, as you read these recordings of Pensatia, repetition is not important. As an apprentice must learn over and over every lesson in trade or schooling until it becomes a conscious part of him, so do all the books of the Masters dwell on the Law, over and over. To the uninitiated it will seem only a rehash, to the serious student he will know the Master is speaking direct to him.

"So readers, which are you? The serious seeker, or the shallow reader who ever says: 'This is the same old story repeated.' It is for you to decide. One must practice and ponder and obey before the inner wisdom is accessible to him. Like the steady hammering on a nail finally attains its objective, so does repetition pull man into the inner chamber of awakening and seeking. *Seek, enter and learn.*

"When one realizes there is a Path, from then on a reverence, a zeal beyond compare, comes to the true student. Henceforth he is dedicated, and will walk the Path knowing when ready, the Master will appear. He is prepared to face the initiations esoteric. Yes, when one knows his course is set to the High Mountain of the Rose of Life, ever within his heart's consciousness walks the beloved Guru, who softens the harsh flame of the crucibles and aids in the transmutation of base metals into gold. The Master ever protects and shows the way up to the Cosmic heights. Yes, you who seek and find the Path, persevere through the long dark night of the soul, for the Stone and Elixir shall be yours. The affinity of earth and heaven shall reveal the oneness of all creation. All races will come alive and warm to your heart. Brothers of one blood, you will become a citizen of Heaven and Earth. From the ramparts of Cosmic dimensions you can see both far and near and roam at will the twelve strata of consciousness. Yet before this may be realized, the student must pass through all the labyrinths of the Path. He must earn attainment step by step as he acquaints himself with the terra firma of each stratum of consciousness. The boot training is severe, yet ever the neophyte is protected and aided by the Masters, those venerable Brethren of the White Lodge.

"The Path, starting in the foothills of man's consciousness, carries one up to the supernal heights of Master and God illumination. In mathemetical law and order the Master takes one through every degree of initiation and attainment until, duly prepared, man is at-one on all planes. He knows because his experience has led him from 'Dante's Hell' into 'Paradise.' He knows even as the Essene, Jesus, that heaven indeed is within man himself. He has pierced the veil of maya's illusions and the duality of matter and risen from the Cross of Matter to the Mountain of Light.

"On the Path, the Master walks with each disciple who has earned his presence, near or far. One can commune with the Master. All his wisdom, compassion and infinite love goes with the obedient student, even over the portals of death. Verdant green and ever fresh, the elixir of life everlasting! Upward, and white the Master's aura and presence which leads the dedicated disciple to the Holy Grail. The

Master lives, never forget that. Seek and you will find him.

"Now in this Space Age and the Aquarian voltage pouring down upon all, man must sip of the Holy Grail or be petrified into a living death. Every man creates the door which leads one to the Path, or stifles the call — the urge to know. Man himself is his own executioner. He is master or slave. All have the equal power to choose. As one chooses, so starts his evolution or devolution. The Path alone is the savior of mankind, leading one to cosmic consciousness and God attunement. God, the Absolute, pours His Light down through the Path to mankind. To those who follow and obey and experience the Light, in time become Masters, and hence guide their disciples over the Path to Cosmic initiation. Only through and by the Master does man softly climb the arduous Path to the Most High Mountain.

"Pensatia," now the Master spoke softly. Yet in virile resonance his words vibrated strong out to me. "You who seek the Path with humble, open heart, gird your loins, tighten your cordelier, take and master the first step; the next one will be easier. Yet never push yourself beyond each step. One must be victor of one step at a time. To try to jump ahead or take in others, ere the first is mastered, only leads man to a dead end. Foolish is man to seek a short cut, for there is none. Brave man of dauntless courage, have faith, obey and follow through the dark night, the crucibles, the cross. Victory will be yours. You will rise, resurrected in your Body of Light. While in your earthly temple, you will sip with the Masters and serve in fulfillment of your Cosmic mission. You will love and be loved by your Cosmic affinity. The time will come when the Path will enfold you as a lover enfolds his beloved. Yes, the time arrives when the Path means more than breath itself. At the ultimate journey's end one finds 'Pilgrim's Rest' — that abiding place within one's consciousness. Yes, Pensatia, students and readers — the wisdom of Buddha, the power of Krishna, the love of the Essene, Jesus, the light of the Holy Grail, that everlasting Elixir and Stone — are yours to use for God and humanity. You stand liberated on the Mountain Top, there where your Master says, 'Well done, good and faithful disciple,' there where the heat and toil of the crucibles are no more, where human tears are transmuted into the joy and fulfillment of cosmic consciousness and oneness with all life. Yes, after the leveling process — the grueling mining into the depths of oneself the initiate experiences — one perceives and knows that Light which all the Avatars speak of. Yes, at the Mountain Top the disciple has arrived. He has traveled the Way of the Masters and won.''

Now, as I listened and journeyed upon the ancient road, that beloved communion and serenity of the Master's presence warmed my heart. I thought: If man could but know what he misses living only in the loam of matter, enslaved by his objective senses and the duality of maya. If one only realized how futile and empty the man, or woman, who seeks not the Way of the Masters — how blasé one gets following "the way of all flesh".....

"Now in this Aquarian Age man must enter the Path or be pulled back into his self-made negative karma. Search and find this Path deep in the center of your heart. Enter the outer gate as it opens to you, and in ripeness of time the Holy Master will call you to discipleship. You will follow trustfully as he guides you through the initiations of earth, water, fire and air. You will know through experience the music of the spheres; the white magic of Cosmic law will make anew your life. The awareness of nature's deepest mysteries, and the wonders of higher dimensions of learning and seeing, will be yours. You will sing, work and walk evermore with the Master and use the Stone and Elixir for Humanity.

"The Path shines its beacon light out to all shipwrecked humanity, regardless of race, creed or earthly states. It invites all who seek soul consciousness to search and find the Way of the Masters. The Path is no coy effervescent road of changing values. It is indeed that straight and narrow Path leading to peace and brotherhood. It is serpentine, yet direct in its course to the Mount of Azùl. On it the neophyte becomes master of each step. As he progresses upward, he attains vibrational and inner awakening of the chakras, thus attuning with his infinite heritage. From the first conscious awareness of the Path, the neophyte knows he has chosen truly. Dedicated from then on, the student works with zeal and obedience to the Cosmic tutelage. He knows when he is ready the Master will come. He knows, too, it is a long journey up. One is pioneering into the unknown within man's depths. Yet, he knows also, each obedient step brings its inner and outer rewards and soul awareness.

"The Path starts in obscurity but blossoms into Cosmic splendor. Only on the self-conscious Path of the Masters does man create the Stone and Elixir of fabled fame. From the beginning to the end all is of infinite plan by the Creator for the development and liberation of man's mortal karma. The neophyte must walk the outer while searching for the within. One's body and mind must be purified of all negative dross that the Light of the Living Rose shine through his chakras in service and creative power out to life."

As we sat, and the Master explained, I have pointed out the relative outline of the Path, ever soaring up the Cosmic altitude.

"Rest thy pen, Pensatia, until I meet you in the next chapter."

So closes the ninth record of this book of "The Path."

❀ Chapter Ten

"ONE MAY become conscious of the Path early or late in life. Of course, it is to man's advantage that he awaken in early manhood.

"Cosmic tutelage in youth is most conducive to entering the outer portal. Yet know, only application, obedience and heart devotion to the Path can turn the key within to the realization of the Way of the Masters. The desire must be so strong in the student or seeker of the Path that no outer impediment can dampen the search.

"All lesser things will be discarded for this great journey with the Masters. Unless this is so, even if one gains admittance to the outer temple, he will be spewed out. And until he comes as the Prodigal Son, only then will he again obtain access to the Way. So search, find and enter. And once your feet have touched the soil of the Path, follow through. Thus only is the High Mountain won.

"With each degree of learning man acquires personal intimacy and understanding of Cosmic law. Thus earthly attainment to the Living Masters, visible and invisible, becomes more certain.

"Every neophyte in time must become a Divine Alchemist. In the crucibles of fire, earth, air and water, he learns to bring forth the Stone and the Elixir. He becomes at the appointed moment the Magus of White Magic, the wielder of the Wand of Isis. The staff of justice and power is given him to use for mankind. As the inner centers, or chakras, awaken and revolve towards the Golden Flame he becomes self-conscious on all planes and dimensions of living. No longer is he bound by earth — but all points of the compass, earthly and heavenly, are his to explore. He journeys at will the Way. The Masters promise this to all disciples who persevere and obey.

"The Path has no favorites. One earns each victory and attainment by actual experience and inner initiation into the deeper mysteries. One becomes magnetized in the Cosmic voltage of the Creative Word. Earth and heaven become mated in the music of the spheres. One senses the divine mandate back of all creation. Step by step the neophyte walks in the Way of the Masters. Learning balance on all points of the triangle, he tastes and drinks of the nectar of the Gods. The song of life enfolds one in its Cosmic rhapsody. One's consciousness finds God, the Creator, alive in all His creation. He sees the ignorance, the blackness of ever-changing maya's mist, pass into the immortality of Light.

"The Path liquidates and levels all experience into the wisdom of the ages. At the summit of the Most High Mountain, the disciple receives all and hence carries back to earth dimensions the message of life everlasting. His aura scintillates with the golden ray of the illumined soul consciousness. He walks as the prince of Ra. He is afire with Cosmic splendor. The Word now speaks from every action. Love flows like a magnet out to the wide world. Mortal man is equipped with all the chakras which, when awakened, will take him to all dimensions infinite. One's Soul consciousness is his passport to the Living Word which lifts one to the current of the Masters. Only by walking the Path of the Masters can this come to pass. All the Avatars, the great men of immortality, walked and won the illuminated heart.

"The time has arrived when the Cosmic gong sounds out

157

proclaiming the march of man to this ancient esoteric Path of the Masters. In that greater silence within the Cathedral of the Soul one must worship, or perish as did Atlantis of old. In that meditative Hall of Silence one in time hears the eternal sound of the Word — that creative sound which heals, purifies and lifts man's consciousness to the holy mountain of soul awareness. Yes, Pensatia, man has the keys to the kingdom within his own being. Only there will be found the Shangri-la man is ever seeking. The true patriots of America, those immortal souls of America's birth, their voices shall be heard again, and man will find the Hesperians of Phylos the Thibetan a reality. Man cannot find the inner Path of the Rose until he passes the outer barriers. The Master knows when one is ripe for the awareness of the experience of such. When this happens, one is truly taken by the Master as a pupil. Henceforth, whether he knows it or not, he is never alone. Ever in the shadows stands the Guru, teaching, aiding, guarding one's steps up to the Mountain of Light.

"Actual knowing of the Path comes to each in a different way. It is an initiation of stupendous value. Until one is aware and has conscious experience of the real Path, which is embedded in the outer temples and wisdom schools, he lives only on the outskirts. His learning is likened to one who knows the contents of all books yet experiences nothing. No one can hand the wisdom to any one. Each must through dedication and obedience push open the inner door himself.

"Many linger ever in the outer portals, seeking the material and social aspect. The serious study and application has no meaning for them. Those foolish ones soon expel themselves, and they drift back into the illusions and duality of earth's escapism, forever living in the shadows. For them the Path, the High Mountain, doesn't exist. Because

they never had the guts to dare, and be silent, they decry
the Path of the Masters. Thus are they enslaved to their
own negative karma. All such can not survive in the Aquarian Age — the golden renaissance of man's soul liberation.

"The pulsating life of the Path is lost to the weaklings
— those Judas who sell their birthright for gold; those
curiosity seekers of magic and occult powers; those who
seek quick results without earning such in the crucibles and
Way of the Cross. The Path is never visible to such. And if
by chance they do get in by proxy, or with drugs, or through
forcing, they instantly are exterminated as if by lightning.
For only the pure in heart may know the real Path of the
Masters. It is futile for man to seek gold unless he seeks to
become an Alchemist, a disciple of the Master's Path. It is
futile to be wedded to tinsel and maya's falseness and at-
tempt to achieve cosmic consciousness. It can't be done. It
is of no avail attending lectures, reading occult books, unless one enters the Path and walks the way upward.

"After listening, and reading, one must act. Book knowledge and intellect is not enough, and can never be the passport to the Golden Dawn and the Elixir. All Masters and
Avatars in some incarnation had to start as the neophyte
and earn the initiations which lead to their divine destiny
and Cosmic mission. Such was not handed to them on a
silver platter. This luminous Path within man and earth is
indistinguishable, save to those whose hearts have awakened. To those seeking only material laurels or occult
phenomena, they can never reach the Most High Mountain.

"Often the most zealous disciples, those trusted channels of the Master Path, travel incognito. The eminence of
their work and service to the Path of the Masters, call often
for service unrecognized by the masses. Yet in the archives

of Akasha they shine forth as Knights of the Living Rose, the alchemists of the Stone and Elixir. Often such are bound to be lone crusaders on their Cosmic mission. Yet know, this is only for a season.

"Often one is lifted into fame and riches. Yet these mean nothing to the disciple. He accepts earthly honors with modesty and thanks to God and man and the Lords of Karma. Always sooner or later the disciple receives his just dues. Be it art, pen, music or science or just living, the true disciple of the Path of the Masters reaps green harvest here and now, or when he passes through transition.

"No walker of the Path esoteric is left without the love and protection of his beloved Master. And when the great initiation comes, the Master is right there guiding him over the River Styx. Welcomed he is into the White Lodge and the Golden Dawn. His loved ones meet him, and he gravitates to all the deep desires of his heart and soul never realized on Earth. Yes, here or in transition the disciple reaps his rewards in full. And when he returns to earth life, all life and heaven will be at his service. Yet ever in receiving all he gives all. Having everything within himself he needs nothing. Thus every good thing flows to him. Yes, Pensatia," affirmed H, "this Path is laden with justice, grace and Cosmic bounty personified."

Now the Master turned and bade me follow.

We came to an intersection where four roads branched out from the Path of the Masters. Each one presented some aspect of man-made cults, religious beliefs as well as fleshly pleasures. The Path continued straight ahead. Standing firmly on its golden soil, we paused.

"Pensatia," the Master spoke, "many reach too far on the Path, then compare these out-roads with the Way of the Masters. The courageous go on up to the Most High

Mountain. The weak ones leave the Path and try one by-road after the other, mastering none. They throw away their birthright for 'fool's gold.' Yet God and the Master never condemns. Karmic reaction and Cosmic law prevails. Those who walk away will settle the score in some other incarnation. They will have to start as a neophyte again and make the inner initiations which they missed or passed up. Remember, it is the Creative Mandate that all mankind must in some incarnation, take this esoteric journey and attain the Mount of Illumination. Such is repeated over and over in this recording. Assimilate, and when once you put your feet on the Path, turn not away.

"To compare is wise. All must at the right point compare. But never get off base. That is, know that nought of earth or heaven can compare with the esoteric Path of the Masters. It alone can come through all earthly comparisons with victory and immortality. It alone can weather all adversity and karmic reaping. It alone can exemplify the Way to the Living Rose and life everlasting. Why? Because it rises above and beyond all earth glamour or human seeking. It is grounded in the blood, sweat and fire of the crucibles of mastership.

"No earthly taint or materialism spawns its birth. It is the one pure Path of endeavor and tutelage that brings one to their true Master and oneness with the God of their heart. These by-paths, or cults, one should and must investigate. Much light flows through their portals. See and bless the constructive, the elevating. Yet never leave the Path of the Masters — that golden dawn of the Living Rose. All else fades in comparison when one knows the real Path. It alone can live into immortality and initiate man to Cosmic altitude.

"In ripeness of time, all such by-paths will give way to

this majestic Path of the Masters. All life will gravitate to its holy portal. Nature and man, beasts, the whole wide world will be in harmony with the music of the spheres. Then and then only will the renaissance of the Golden Age of Aquarius be a living reality on Earth. Thus will the Masters once more walk with mankind, and the invisible become visible."

Now as the Master paused I beheld many persons basking in the scintillating light of the glamorous by-paths, sensed their reaching out to short cuts, only to fail, for there is none. I beheld the floundering ones trying all the flamboyant rites aimed to bring quick contact with occult powers and the Masters. Saw I the disappointment and finally cynical failure. They all ended in a dead end.

"This happens when man leaves the Cosmic Path of the Masters," H commented on my thoughts. "Such are the vagabonds of mysticism, who try every will-o'-the-wisp way, and master none.

"The shining Path of the Masters is the Cosmic liberator of civilization," H continued. "Its authenticity is etched forever in the records of Akasha. The Venerables of the White Lodge guard its sacred wisdom. Naught can walk and win the High Mountain save those who earn victory in the Alchemist Laboratory. No spurious seeker of the Way ever meets the Master. Quality, not quantity is written over every true temple of the Living Rose and Golden Dawn. Not intellectual achievement or scientific honor. But the purity of the heart, and the faith that moves mountains, steadfast obedience, living a natural life, outgoing and ever seeking the Stone and the Elixir. Only such can penetrate the mysteries of the Holy See."

Now as we communed and strolled along the Path we came to that garden of Cosmic dimension. The soft golden light, the celestial music of the spheres, flowed over and through this most treasured spot of the Path. Sheltering trees with leafed, green sprawling limbs called us to their restful shade. Flowers of all colors grew in spontaneous fashion. Emerald-colored grass grew like smooth velvet while a silver stream in happy ripples undulated through this Garden of Peace. It made me think of "The Door of the Heart," my first contact with this esoteric peace. We continued our talk and relaxed beneath a great spreading tree.

"Always," said H, "the disciple comes here when ready and in this high altitude of garden Master and pupil commune, one with the other. Ask what you will, Pensatia. Know the true answer will be given you."

I pondered. Attar of roses filled the atmosphere. Birds sang and chirped. Love, glorious, universal, seeped through blood and bone. One felt the unity and goodness of all life. I thought of the many questions the uninitiated ask, and even so the ones long on the Path. Thus I throw out the questions as they jump from my mind.

Question: "Why do the Masters veil themselves from the world?"

Answer: "It is people who cast a cloud, keeping the Masters out, not the Master. For every step man takes towards the Master, so does the Master take two. Man himself hides from the Master. As a snake sheds his skin, even so must man shed all that binds him from the Master."

Question: "How can one know if it is the Master speaking — or a fraud?"

Answer: "One knows for the peace, uplift, the calm assurance of his heart telling one. One feels the God presence, the truth whenever the Master speaks. Always the Light of the Holy Ghost, the Living Word, shines through the

Master and blesses the disciple. Yes, one *knows*. Yet to know, one himself must know. If the neophyte or disciple is false, then also is the Master's voice. Remember this."

Question: "Does the Master really come to the disciple of the Rose when transition comes?"

Answer: "That, one can depend on. Never is the Walker of the Path left alone. Even if he has never seen him in life, always, when transition comes one *sees* and feels and *knows* the Master is with him. This can not be unless one has embraced the Path. Yet in orthodox religion, if one truly follows and obeys the Living Christ, He will take the faithful servant in peace over the River Styx. Remember Jesus, the Christed One, is among the greatest of the Masters."

Question: "Will the Masters ever come out in the open and walk with man again?"

Answer: "Yes, without a doubt, when man himself is ready. In the next century a Master man will lead the nation. One tutored on the esoteric way will come, and all the world will feel his power for good."

Question: "Is capital punishment against Cosmic law?"

Answer: "Yes, irrevocably. It will in time be banished. To kill is not Cosmic law."

Question: "What is the Law of Supply?"

Answer: "Contact with the Source, which has endless riches. Through faith and knowing the Law man may acquire all he needs. One only has to be aware, and his 'cup runneth over.' Man himself closes the circuit. Open and partake of God's abundance."

Question: "Did Jesus perform miracles?"

Answer: "Yes, in human eyes he did. Yet to him and the Masters he only used super laws. All miracles are only such, through ignorance of the laws."

Question: "Can man reap riches at once?"

Answer: "The minute the contact is made, so may man receive."

Question: "Will death ever be vanquished?"

Answer "Yes, when man lives according to Cosmic law and partakes of the Stone and Elixir. Death is not what it seems. See beyond maya and know the truth."

Question: "Why the chaos of the world? Will it ever cease?"

Answer: "Yes, when man himself changes. In the full Aquarian Age, science, art, music and medicine will have a spiritual renaissance. Cosmic remedies for healing will have precedence over all else. Man will have attuned himself with the divine center within. Harmony between Nature, Man and Beast will prevail. Yet this can be only by Soul evolution and walking the Path of the Masters. Remember, God or the Masters do not compel. Man is ever free to choose. According to one's choice does man work with his spiritual destiny or against it. Yes God's law is as above below, as below above. There must be that alchemical mating of the two, reducing all to the universal whole."

Question: "Is a Soul Mate a myth or actual fact?"

Answer: "It is a Cosmic and eternal fact. Only when one has liquidated all karmic loves and has received the Alchemical Marriage, can and will the Cosmic and Soul Mate come into one's life. Yes, it is not fiction. Every one has a Soul Mate. Only on the self-conscious Path does man realize that great LOVE and fulfillment which is rightfully his when one is prepared and earns such."

Question: "How does one know and recognize his Mate?"

Answer: "There is that intangible oneness of mind, heart and Soul which one feels and senses. There is an inner knowing that can not be denied. Soul speaks to Soul. Never

165

doubt that this will be, for it is Cosmic law. Soul seeks Soul — man to woman, and woman to man — the two joined in the Alchemical Marriage."

The Master ceased answering questions and passed on up the Path echoing his words back to me.

"Another time, another hour we will meet and finish our 'Journey.'"

So closes this tenth chapter of "The Path."

❀ Chapter Eleven

AGAIN spoke the illustrious Master H:

"The Path has no earth or heavenly barriers. Its luminous brightness shines out for all souls to enter if they will. People themselves create the impediments which bar their entrance. Within their hearts is the Holy Way to the citadel of the living Rose of Life. Through the raising of the kundalini, and the awakening of the sacred chakras, one lifts his consciousness to the thousand-petalled lotus in the head. There the cleavage takes place, and behold, one knows he is a Native of the Light. Henceforth one walks at will in all dimensions of infinite strata. Up, up he climbs to the Most High Mountain of Cosmic Illumination, and achieves yogic at-oneness with God and the Masters.

"Oh, yes, the Path is solid as the Rock of Gibraltar and earth loam. All nature worships at the shrine of God's golden sun, back of the fiery orb which illumines and warms our earth. All living things thrive, grow and bloom in lush colors. The animals, unspoiled, roam at will in God's primeval forests. Only man dares to deny his birth into divinity and wars and battles with his brethren. In desperation and agnosticism he flouts the very reality of a Path, and boldly states there is no God, that the Essene, the Christed Jesus, is a myth, an old tale of story tellers. He puts blindness in his eyes, and ever walks past the age-old outer portals of the Rosae Crucis. He sips only of maya's illusions and ends up feeding on the husks. Yet, when like the Prodigal Son, he seeks the esoteric Path of the Masters, the Path welcomes him, and he starts the boot training for his mystical initiation.

"The Path little by little exposes the spurious, the tinsel of maya's illusions, and proves to man's inner senses that God is, the Masters are, and the soul exists. Through initiation and the lighted heart man walks within, with his God and the Master who guides him onward to the afflatus of life everlasting. This is no idle talk, but cold reality. There is a mathematical formula which is exact, unfailing. Accept it, live it, and all may find the Elixir and the Stone. This is given to all who enter and follow the Path of the Masters. Yet one must seek to find. One must dare, do and be silent, and yet exemplify the Light which he receives as he wins step by step the way to the Cosmic mountain."

As the Master discoursed I felt anew the majesty, the mercy and love of the Creator. As the Word made possible for man the way back to the Source, how plainly did the Path reveal man's destiny in the Aquarian Age. How privileged one is to journey on the age-old Path of the Masters. All mundane joy, all world wealth, seems worthless without the light of the Golden Dawn. Barren and empty man's heart unless awakened by the Fire of Isis. Cold the intellect unless warmed by the heart's flame. Earth life unless mated and wed with the Word and higher dimensions is void of wisdom. Earth, air, water and fire must be traversed and transmuted into their divine essence. Thus only can man know himself.

167

"Yes, Pensatia," the Master interrupted my thoughts, "man can and will redeem himself from the shackles of ignorance and material objectivity. He will prove to himself the soul and the interior state of consciousness. Extra sensory perception will be a common happening. Thought transference, psychic projection and communion in all dimensions and planes will come into its own. All this will be as man seeks and enters the Way of the Masters. After the boot training, the working in the crucibles, the victorious passing of the initiations, the walking through the dark night of the soul and out into the light of the Golden Dawn, one reaches the evergreen garden where one may bask in the infinite variety of Cosmic stream and wooded coolness and fragrance of attar of roses. There in the transcendent color of flower, and the glorious plumage and song of birds, there in that peace profound of inner sanctuary, one may journey at will and recharge one's body and mind through attunement with God and the Masters. Here one may rest from his mundane toil and sip of the Elixir. One may relax on the white lily 'Field of Ardath' and see clear over the horizons of light. One may hear the hum of the AUM and feel the oneness with earth and heaven. Yes, one may slumber on the hearth of the Gods and be aware, refreshed, regenerated, and bring back to earth vibrations wisdom gathered in Cosmic Garden. Such are some of the many oases of the Path of the Masters. At every level of attainment man reaps the Master's blessing. Man earns and receives his just due. Through faith, application, love and service, one trudges on, facing the lessons of the crucibles, ever preparing for the initiations of earth, fire, air and water, and the crowning initiation on the Most High Mountain."

Now a smoky haze settled upon the Path. Even the Master's presence was veiled in the thickness of mist. There was an austere loneliness, an empty, all-gone feeling, as if man were caught in an arid desert of vast mystery. Out of the blankness the beloved voice of the Master spoke, saying, "Pensatia, and all who walk the Path, fear not the drab desert-like mist which covers one on the Path. Walk on in faith and obedience and soon you will have crossed the barren stretch. It is only the stagnant aftermath of collective negation of man that one must pass through and liquidate forever. Remember and walk on, else the astral pull will keep you chained to your self-made earth cross. When the disciple reaches this crisis, he does not fight it or recognize the gloom. He just walks on, knowing the Light is. The Master stands by even though you cannot see, hear or sense him. Command with your inner strength that this pass and you come out beyond the bog and turmoil of life, and see straight beyond the negation of maya into the Light of the Rose.

"The uninitiated, those vested only in the material — those of worldly ego and bigoted narrow closed minds — they pass by the Path, call it a fantasy; that which they have no knowledge of, is not. Such are chained in their self-made prison of stagnation. Not until they choose to break the chains of ignorance will and can they become aware of a bright new world within themselves. Only the Path of the Masters gives first-hand to the neophytes and postulants the secret door that proves ESP, the reality of the soul, and the inner signature of every mundane thing. Its lofty vibrations pouring down from the Most High Mountain ignites the rose fire in man's heart and starts one on the holy pilgrimage of cosmic consciousness. It is a natural growth, a gradual opening of the psychic centers, a steady awareness of one's soul powers. It is a faith justified, a fulfillment of God's plan and creative fiat for all humanity.

"Outside the Path man is an exile from his divine heritage. Like driftwood he knows not where he will land. All the beauty and glory of life he sails by, not realizing his only anchor is within one's inner consciousness. In his ignorance, man is chained to matter rather than being master. In pitiful slavery to maya's illusions and the materialism of the temporal-objective, he lives in poverty of mind and action. Only the esoteric Path of the Masters and the Living Rose can bring man into the everlasting wealth of the Golden Dawn and the oneness with his soul power. See, Pensatia, the light that flows upon man as he journeys upward, even when sorrow and the travail of the cross lies heavy on one! On this Path, man *finds* the courage, the strength to press on. With joyful heart, one knows that this too will pass, and the High Mountain will surely be won. Man feels the Master's love and presence through all his journey. He hears the music of the spheres. Rugged be the steps which take him to the Elysian heights! Yet in obedience and faith he knows he will make it. Yes, the Path is, God is, the Masters are!"

As the Master H conversed, and we journeyed on, the Path seemed to wrap us in its maternal heart. A soothing, yet invigorating atmosphere quivered in the air like a scintillating jewel. Darkness merged into light. All nature, desert, sea, woods and valleys, all reflected the Golden Flame of the Creator. Earth was wedded with heaven. The soul of man bore witness to the Oversoul, to Ra, the Sun God, to the Jehova of Sinai, to the Essene, the Christed Jesus. All earth was a symphony of life, joyous, creative with the fire of the Most High Mountain.

"Such," spoke H, "is the inevitable glory of the Aquarian Age. Such is the mandate of the Cosmic Hierarchy. As above, below, as below, above. Only man himself can delay the glory of the New Age. All the values of the past must be venerated, the foundational laws of the Cosmic be cherished. Yet ever man must pioneer for humanity's use and soul benefit all the wonders of space. The planets must be known and man must learn of those greater in wisdom than the earthlings. All the lost powers of Atlantis must be regained and utilized for the blessing of mankind. This can only be by man entering and walking the Path of the Masters. Otherwise the sweep of the Aquarian Light will, as lightning, flash man into the debris of exile. Only the esoteric student can withstand the vibrational power of Light that the Aquarian Waterpitcher is, and will pour upon the earth.

"So, Pensatia, it behooves man to awake and drink from the Cosmic fount. When one enters the Path, in time realization reveals the heart center as the *Way* to the Masters. It is a blending process, a unification of the infinite and the finite. When both merge then there is a wholeness of spirit in earth, heaven and man. This is the goal of the Creator, to quicken man's liberation from mundane subjection, and to open one's spiritual arteries that heavenly manna circulate through his chakras out to life and humanity. It is through the Path esoteric that man becomes aware of the God within and the presence of the Hierarchal Masters. Yes the call echoes far and near, sounding the gong for man to arise and journey the Path upward. To ignore the call sets man's evolution back many lives.

"After one emerges from the dark night of the soul, which all must pass through at some point of the Path, all becomes brighter and, the 'bluebird' sings most gloriously for one. The goal of the Alchemist is to transmute all base metals to the Elixir and Philosopher's Stone. One feels rich

171

even though bereft of all earthly gains. He knows that in the Source is every thing. When once aware of this great truth, man then has only to contact the reservoir of supply and ask and it is his. One depends no more on the world but looks only to the Living Word. Yet through what channel his supply comes, is not for man to say. His part in life is to walk the Path and fulfill his earth obligations, and listen, and obey his call to his mission. All that one lets go of on the Path he knows will return to him cup running over.

"The Path is like a rich mine. Each must discover the gold within himself first, and then out into the world. So you see, Pensatia, the Path is not a gossamer myth, but is practical and down to earth, and is the key to the deeper mysteries of life. It prepares one to know first-hand all the truth, and natal atmosphere and influence of the planets. It reveals man himself is captain of his soul and that all is sired from the Creator."

As he spoke, soft rose flush of heavenly dew rained upon the Path, refreshing, purifying, and from the High Mountain the Golden Flame of regeneration and life mingled with the dew of the rose, and all earth sprouted with new glory. Nature sang as it were with the birds of the air.

"Yes," spoke H, "as above below, as below above, naught can keep the overflow of light from descending and impregnating Earth. God's infinite design shall prevail. Man's soul shall become king, and man again will walk with God and the Masters of the White Brotherhood. The purification of Earth is taking place; the bitter karma of world and personal causation is being liquidated and purged in the crucibles of initiation and the air of the New Age. Those who are still happy in their ignorance and materialistic, domestic and aimless existence, cannot survive of their own making. They pass by the Path to fulfillment and life everlasting."

As he, the Master, conversed, a heavy shadow darkened the face of the Earth. Seen from the vantage point of the Path esoteric, it was as if the Golden Flame from the Most High Mountain was dimmed by the masses, who flaunted past the aged Path of the Masters. It was as if God's creatures had turned against their Creator — the Love Father of the World. I, too, felt the sadness, their turning away from their rich heritage. It was as if Heaven and Earth groaned in the travail of man's unholy killing of his divinity.

Suddenly the dark shadow passed. The ripple and stir of the silver waters of life flowed by and lifted us on its crest of silver wave. And as suddenly we were in Cosmic Garden high in the ramparts of infinite dimension. There we relaxed in the shade of a spreading tree. In natural abandon, yet in beautiful harmony, birds, flowers, trees blended in song and color, scintillating and vivid beyond earth description.

Such is one of the many rewards of man's esoteric journey. This Garden, as all Cosmic books relate, is the outer reflection of that Peace Profound within man's heart. All the beauty of the within comes to birth without, in this fourth dimensional Garden of Allah. Here abideth that close attunement with nature, God and the Masters. What melody, the whisper of the wind moving upon the grass and the variegated colors and flowers! The gay, yellow, red and blue winged birds, all seemed alive with a scintillating aura of vibrational glow which lighted all like a many splendored lamp. One felt renewed in every fiber of being. Mind and and heart were one in thought and action. It was as if all Akasha, Heaven itself, poured all the wisdom of the ages down and through us.

Now an amber haze settled upon the Garden. It was as if

the hush of all the Garden made obeisance to that intangible presence of the Creator and the Living Word.

"Come, Pensatia, we leave," spoke H.

Arising, we journeyed away from the transcendent oasis, and came walking back into earth climate again. Yet even so we carried the Path within our heart. From the first step to its climactic height on the Most High Mountain it burned like a brilliant star. A flame from the Golden Dawn.

As H bade me aparting, his farewell words were:

"Yes, Pensatia, the Path is the alpha and omega of the way to the Rose of Life."

✿ Chapter Twelve

Now as I pen this last chapter of "The Path" a sadness prevails and also a deep joy. The Master and the Path encompass my consciousness like the overtones of the AUM resounding from the temple of the heart. I hear the gong from the Living Word ring out. The Path pulsates that transcendent power of Light. It rolls out to life golden bright and at its apex in all its glory is the Most High Mountain, the crowning victory of the Way of the Masters.

In recording "The Path" the Master has made plain the overtones and undertones. The Cosmic reflection of the Light of the Word is revealed by the presence of the Guru. The cadence and echo of the Holy Grail emanates a glow like a firefly every step of the Way. To witness and walk this Path is the greatest privilege of man.

Now Master H did walk with me to that high edifice, that profound pinnacle of the Path, the Most Lofty Mountain of Rose and Lotus fame. There from Cosmic altitude we scanned the beginning, and now the culminating victory

174

of man as he stepped into the awareness of life everlasting. A thousand bells from man's inner temple pealed out. Behold, his Body of Light stood bright behind his physical vehicle.

Now the Master H spoke out to me. As I listen, so I record.

"When man earns and becomes conscious of his Soul, the Body of Light is henceforth the captain of his earthly journey. From then on the physical body is the faithful servant of man's Divine Self. Until this happens, man is driftwood on the Sea of Maya.

Soul awareness cannot be attained intellectually, or through the reading of books. It must be born in the fires of the crucibles, through the initiations of earth, water, fire and air. Nature must open her heart and give man her innermost secrets. Man must come under the Aquarian spray and be baptized in the waters of life everlasting. The Cosmic mandate is: To receive the Philosopher's Stone and Elixir man must become conscious of his Soul Body, and thus triumph over maya's illusions.

"The purpose of this book, recorded by Pensatia, my amanuensis, is to ignite the search in man and to show him the Way of the Masters. All Avatars, all esoteric wayshowers of the White Brotherhood, have walked this Path and won the victory and realization of their Body of Light. Hence, at so-called death, already at home in the Soul Body, they walk into heaven having already known it on earth. So you see, readers, this intimate journey with Pensatia is only I, your friend, coming close to you, speaking from the heart, sharing with you who read the ramparts and infinite design for man.

"As you read, ponder, dig deep within your heart for the entrance to the Way of the Masters. Let nothing dim your search. And when you enter as a neophyte, dedicate your all to the Light of the Rose. The Path becomes clear only as man obeys, and braves the crucibles, and prepares with diligence to face his esoteric initiations. Mankind is getting close to the outpouring of the Aquarian Waterpitcher. Vibrant and potent are the Cosmic vibrations flowing earthward. Man must adjust or perish.

"Now, Pensatia, here at the close of our journey, let us tarry in that Cathedral of the Soul, where man may lift his consciousness into that peace and wisdom profound. In the silence of infinite attunement, one may listen to the Hierarchal Masters as they speak from the Cosmic rostrum. One may abide in the symphony of the music of the spheres. The silence and voice of the Word resounds throughout the great vaulted Cathedral. In humble seeking seat yourself before the altar of the heart's flame. There free yourself of all earthly thoughts. Let the baptism of the rose dew clear your earthly body of all impurities. Kindle your soul light that you may read Akasha at will."

Now the Master's countenance shone with the luster of the rose. He held in his hand a tiny sparrow and spoke in that magnetic flow of love.

"Behold this lovely bird, Pensatia. Behold the All-Seeing Eye, watching, caring."

Even as he spoke, the hand of the Father reached down and lifted the bird in the hollow of His hand.

"Even so does the Almighty take care of man. Even so does the Master ever protect and bless the Disciple of the Path."

Now a great blackness descended on the Path of Azùl. "Pensatia," came H's voice through the darkness, "see you naught?"

"Yes," I answered, "I see a streak of golden light."

"It is well," he answered. "All true disciples see this golden beam through all the darkest night. Others see only blackness; hence they leave the Path. Their faith is not stable. Their inner sight fails to know Light is ever. They succumb to mundane darkness. Thus they eliminate themselves from the Path. For without faith to see and know beyond the night, they cannot journey on.

"Pensatia," and now his voice was stern and vibrant with Cosmic strength, "heed not the darkness when all seems naught. Hold to that gleam of golden ray which thy faith will show thee. Tramp through the ebb tide, sense and feel the oncoming wake of harvest, sense the beacon flash from the Most High Mountain. Heed not the physical weakness which overtakes one on the esoteric journey. Heed not the inertia that would kill thy dedication. Arise and give the battle cry of thy innards and push through the obstacles of thy lesser self. As you obey, when hungry, without world gold, without love or home, empty and alone, and walk on — as surely as night follows day, and dawn blossoms from darkness, even so will all you thought lost be returned to you. The evergreen of the High Mountain will pasture you. No longer will you feed on the husks of life, but eat and drink you will from the royal table of God the Father and the Masters. For behold, the Path contains the pure gold of the soul, even so all the treasures of earth. As above, so will earth and man reflect and know the glory of God and the Masters. From neophyte and on to discipleship and to the victory of Master, man shall be of the White Brethren and cross the bridge to the Hierarchal Mount of the Living Rose and Golden Dawn. There, in the crowning consciousness of Cosmic awareness, men of super wisdom will walk the earth and create the Mecca of the Aquarian Age. Yet before this comes, man must enter the esoteric road and

177

earn the Jewel of the Lotus — that blessed oneness with all life."

The Master paused. In humble majesty he looked upon me. His eyes were filled with sorrow for the ignorance and negative self-made karma of man. His very heart spoke from his eyes.

"Pensatia, how can man sell his birthright for 'fool's gold?' "

Now the light of his aura beamed out and down into the darkness of man's ignorance. With the resounding flow of AUM, his fingertips touched earth's loam. And the Word, alive from his throat, resounded over the Living Rose. With the Waters of Life, he baptized man. All who were ready, all those seeking, were ignited to enter and walk the Kings Highway to the High Mountain, its lofty peak rose high in Cosmic citadel. And a gentle breeze, yet quick in action, fanned man's inertia to life. Such is the impact and influence of the Hierarchal Masters, those of the White Lodge, those who bring the Light from the East, those who shoot the Cosmic arrow into man's heart, those who sound the drum of the Word out to all humanity. Such is the Path the way-shower of the Aquarian Age, the lighthouse to man's liberation from maya.

Now the Master H turned to me, saying,

"Thus closes this book of 'The Path.' Pensatia, lay up thy pen and rest until another recording I tender thee."

I obeyed. The pages pressed close, one to the other, and await man's opening.

. . .

. .

.

The Golden Dawn

DEDICATED TO EUCLID

My Friend and Co-Worker

Prelude

IN THE silence of the heart's temple walked the Master H. Came he with a new assignment.

I felt the strength and wisdom from his aura golden-lighted. In his hand he held my Cosmic pen, saying,

"Take it, Pensatia, and write as I tell you of 'The Golden Dawn, its Meaning and Attainment.'"

"So do I obey," came my answer.

"Well spoken, Pensatia. Seat yourself here and relax in the peace profound of thy heart's temple."

Even as he spoke my consciousness was transported to the Isle of Samos. There by the sea of life, there in a grove of tall and stately pines we sat upon the green grass of Earth's loam. The ancient aroma of attar of roses filled the atmosphere. The resounding tone of music of the spheres echoed softly through the trees.

"Here," spoke H, "we will meet each day until the recording of 'The Golden Dawn' is finished."

Arising, his parting words ignited in my heart:

"Obey, Pensatia. Let my message live for man."

Thus ends this prelude to a new esoteric journey with the Master H.

❀ Chapter One

I T WAS a misty gray day, November 2, 1967, when again
I made my contact with the Master on the Isle of Samos.
On a spiraled path of golden luster he led me as of yore
to the green grove of pines. There by the waters of life, re-
clining on the emerald cushions of nature, was the Master.
He arose and bade me be seated.

We relaxed in profound silence, a silence pithy with
Cosmic impact. It was as if all heaven and Akasha's archives
were ready to burst their sacred wisdom through my pen
of Azùl. A new regenerating flow of life poured strength
and joy within my heart.

With pen in hand and writing scroll, in earnest awareness I heed the Master's words:

"Pensatia," spoke the venerable Master H, "the Golden
Dawn has been venerated through many sagas of life. Its
vaulted wisdom has graced many a book, yet ever its
mystery Light lay hidden from men. Few have realized the
Golden Dawn is in man. No book, however great, can catch
that infinite radiance, save man himself.

"Esoteric books can only ignite man's heart to make the
search within. The Cosmic meaning of the Golden Dawn
is the luminous Rose of Life, that divine glow, that inner
white magic which liberates man's consciousness in spiritual
union with his Creator and one's earth life.

"Here on the Isle of Samos the Golden Dawn permeates
the atmosphere. No one who has not contacted the Golden
Dawn within the heart center can transport himself here,
save the Masters bring him. One can do so only when his
mission calls for such.

"You, Pensatia, have journeyed here to record this book
which is to be published for humanity. Here you shall see
clear, and shall transmit my words as you receive.

"Now what do you feel as you sit with me on the Isle of Samos?"

"My feeling, Master H," I answered, "is a most peaceful, yet a transcendent lifting up of consciousness. It is as if I am anchored in a golden glow which spreads through Cosmic and earthly dimensions. A feeling of knowing and having access to Akasha's records. A feeling of the goodness, beauty and love pervading all life. It is a feeling vibrant with meaning, yet steadfast, balanced and harmonious."

"Good," spoke H. "As you now feel, so must all, in their own time. Now what do you see, Pensatia?"

Answering, I said, "I see far and near, up and down, into the depths and the Alpha and Omega of creation. I see Cosmic truth shining through heaven down to earth. I see the White Brotherhood, the Hierarchal Masters, the Saints and all the denizens of earth walking together serving the Lord — the Living Word. I see the Golden Dawn blessing the Aquarian Age. I see love's sacred mystery lifting man and woman into 'the grand passion immortal;' see the bloom of nature in all its infinite glory communing with man; see man penetrating all the hidden strata of life's meaning, with heart and mind unified in service to God and the Masters. All this I see and more. I see through 'Dante's Hell' to a regained Paradise, see man's Shangri-la a reality."

"Well spoken, Pensatia," said H. "Now what do you hear? Listen and pen."

Obeying, my inner hearing caught the winds of Light, Life and Love wooing the winds of earth and mating, bringing forth the melody of the spheres. "I hear the 'Well done' of the Masters as humanity enters the esoteric path. I hear the bells of cosmic gong proclaiming the Aquarian Waterpitcher pouring out its wisdom for man. I hear the melting of hate and the golden fusion of love pollenizing all earth.

I hear all-new bright joy breathing across the land, stimulating a renaissance of the creative dignity of man. Art, literature and music sounding forth representing the Golden Dawn, which is the blood of the New Age — that immaculate circulation of life which is in man when he becomes aware of such.

"O Master!" I exclaimed, "all this is heard, felt and seen in panoramic Roll of Akasha."

"Yes, this will be" answered H, "yet man must first bring it to pass within himself. God created man a living soul in a body. Until man realizes this and is ruled by his soul wisdom he is naught but a self-glorified zombie, unaware of his divine powers. The Golden Dawn lies hidden from man only because his inner chakras have not awakened, only because he has not learned the Law of the Triangle. The Golden Dawn is that fluid of the Godhead shining, penetrating through man from the Most High Mountain. It is the Elixir and meaning of life, the Living Rose.

"Pensatia, like a ripple of music, light and color the Golden Dawn flows through one's being, lifting the consciousness to Cosmic illumination in relative degrees according to one's attainment. A fusion of inner sight, hearing and feeling takes place. The initiate of the Rose Dew finds in awareness of the Golden Dawn a transcendent regeneration of his whole being. One lives, breathes and acts from a new dimension of altitude. No longer does he walk in darkness, even though it might surround him; he knows the Golden Dawn. Neither Hades, the Black Art, or the negation and duality of maya can enslave the disciple who has attained the Golden Dawn."

As the Master talked my inner senses caught the rapture of God's love for man, the tender touch of that everlasting mercy and grace radiating through the Golden Dawn.

183

The Master reflected the brightness in his aura. Thousands of birds of every hue, brilliant in reds, blues, purples and pinks, sang through the trees of Samos. The green-grassed land was vibrant with earth magnetism. The infinite and finite were wedded, and under the caress of the Golden Dawn gave out a welcome to us.

"Here," continued the Master H, "one in conscious awareness lives and breathes and works in the essence of the rays of the Golden Dawn. Having found it within himself man discovers it in all things from plant to animal. Nature works unconsciously with its golden flow. Primitive man and the ignorant masses, absorbed only in the objective, pass by the Golden Elixir, thus stagnating and becoming enslaved by maya.

"The Golden Dawn has every ingredient of earth and heaven ingrained in its illuminative light. It is the foundation, the source, of the fabled Golden Flame. All creation drinks from its immortal fount. Yet, to be aware of it man must go through the dark night of the soul. One must take the old rugged cross of matter and resurrect one's consciousness into the life-giving aura of Cosmic oneness with all dimensions of experience.

"This cannot be until man becomes the Alchemist. In the crucibles of the Rose man must liberate himself from his karmic chains. The Golden Dawn is that fluid which harmonizes all the lesser in man into the birth of the Golden Dawn within one's self.

"Here on Samos, as we converse, all our inner senses are synthesized into the whole. The very heart of the Creator pours in and through us as we abide on the loam of Samos."

It was so. A quickening of blood, a peace beyond mortal sensing lifted us into the rhapsody of Edenic joy, stabilizing, refreshing. All one's intellectual faculties seemed alive for action. One's heart was a flame of love for every thing. A fragrance of attar of roses in subtle effulgence was as incense to our feelings.

"Pensatia," spoke H, the Master, "remember, the Golden Dawn has two sides — the positive and negative. The Black Art uses the negative power of the Golden Dawn. This is spurious, and destroys all who use it in reverse. True, it may for a time shower one with occult knowledge to perform Black Magic. Yet, ever in the end, the betrayer of the white Golden Dawn dies by that which he has spawned.

"Thus, seekers of the Golden Dawn, be sure you are creating the real Golden Dawn, and not the false. They often travel side by side, the false masquerading as the true. Only under the guidance of a Master and obedience to the God of your heart can the pilgrim of the Rosy Cross know how to steer clear of the spurious Black Dawn.

"The Black Dawn plies every art of occult power for self, and attempts to delude the eager neophyte and young disciple. Only by faith and allegiance to the mandates of the Path can, and will, the student survive the tests in the crucibles and bring forth the Stone and Elixir, the true wisdom of the Golden Dawn.

"Here on the Isle of Samos, Pensatia, our communication is smoother of understanding, making the recording quicker to pen. The atmosphere is ever conducive to attunement between Guru and disciple."

"Yes," I answered, "it is so. I find a clear line, a fluidity of my inner senses which clarify the meaning and attainment of the Golden Dawn."

Continued the Master H: "The Golden Dawn is the real inner school of the Rose. In its golden light the disciples walk, learn, and attain the Wisdom of the Ages. This must be earned by every neophyte of the Way. All must pass

185

the tests of Saturn. All must pass the 'dark night of the soul.' All must become the Divine Alchemist before the Golden Dawn opens fully unto them. Only through supreme dedication of the heart to the esoteric Rose of Life, to the Christus, and to the God of all people can and will mankind find the Golden Dawn. It is the grand portal immortal leading man to the High Mountain and Cosmic Consciousness.

"As one emerges from the 'dark night of the soul' a soft effusion of Light lifts the disciple into a bright new experience of sight, hearing and feeling. A blessed assurance and awareness of the reality of God and the Masters floods one's heart with a gratitude for life. One feels the privilege of serving, giving and receiving.

"In one's first immersion into the Golden Dawn the whole world seems lighted with an auric glow. Humanity, animals, plants — all seem one with the disciple. A pleasing, happy affinity brings one in rapport with all life. All earth seems to sing in adoration of the Creator. One works and acts from a higher dimension and awareness. The inner chakras open and revolve in Cosmic altitude. The disciple realizes he has indeed entered the inner school esoteric. Henceforth, step by step, he must learn to navigate and work in its golden splendor.

"At first the Light is so brilliant, one's sight so keen, the hearing so far and near, one almost feels the splendor is too much to bear. Fear not, one never enters the Golden Dawn unless ready and protected by the Masters. Know this. Take all easy-like and natural. Soon you will be polarized and at home in your expanded consciousness. You will find earth and its various forms of life as transparent and clear as a mirror.

"Never, Pensatia, can one bear witness to the Golden Dawn and not be born anew. Yet to break through to the

Golden Dawn takes much work and obedience to the mandamus of the Rose. One must purify and awaken the chakras
that they may respond to the Masters. The neophyteship
must be spent in life's crucibles. Not until one has proven
one's self through the initiations of earth, water, fire and
air can one qualify for the Golden Dawn.

"There are many books written about the exalted vibrations of color, sound and sight on the esoteric journey. In
recording this book, Pensatia, you will go through each
stage of the Golden Dawn that you may pen in truth the
meaning and attainment of this illustrious Flame.

"The Golden Flame is the bursting of God's effulgence
in man. It is the opening bloom of man's inner chakras. It is
the White Magic of the Magi and of the Essene, Christed
Jesus. It is the Flame of Zoroaster, it is the living Rose of
Life, it is the sacred awakening of the Lotus of India; it is
the immaculate goal of all esoteric students come to fulfillment. It is life everlasting.

"The spurious Golden Dawn is the fake gold of the
Black Art, the tinsel of 'fool's gold.' It destroys all who seek
it, the aftermath of its luster is death.

"The pure Golden Dawn of the Alchemists, of the Rosicrucians, shines out like a golden halo over and through
man, bringing cosmic consciousness and liberation from
maya. It cascades down from the Most High Mountain, pulsating through man's inner centers. The Golden Dawn is
that flame which ignites the love flow in the heart, which
must ever circulate out to life, or man shrivels and dies from
want of use. When attaining the Golden Dawn one must
sleep, breathe, love and create in its Cosmic rays. It is the
purifier of all that is dross in man. It is the ultimate secret
of man's regeneration. It lifts the consciousness into that
vast arena of the Akashic records. One lives in a new cosmic

187

dimension, scintillating with soul power of the Word. It is the union in man of both heaven and earth."

As I listened to the Master H the profound realization became a luminous jewel in my heart. It was as if the whole, wide world was lighted by a heavenly lamp.

"Ah, yes, Pensatia," spoke H, "such is the touch of the Golden Dawn upon one. Out of the darkness of the pit, out of 'Dante's Hell,' the opening curtain of the Golden Dawn bestows upon man true Edenic awakening. One is lifted above his temporal body into the glorious Temple of Light. Henceforth one's soul controls one's actions, one is master of his earth body. When one walks and works and loves in the Golden Dawn his slavery is at an end, maya no longer dominates him. He is one with the song of life, one with nature and with all races of men. Daily he purges the remaining negation still lingering within his subconscious. He is truly on the road to the Most High Mountain.

"The spurious Golden Dawn is the loathsome citadel of the Black Art, those false masters of occult power for selfish goals. The false Golden Dawn allures the weak disciple away from the true. It injects false promises of quick illumination, the promise of material riches and power over others. The end result is disillusion and emptiness, while the true Dawn brings peace profound, inner wisdom and attunement with the Cosmic Masters of the White Brotherhood. It bequeaths courage, love and strength to carry out one's earthly and Cosmic assignments. It creates humility and a grateful heart for one's blessings. Like the alchemists of old, the real Golden Dawn reveals the Mystery Esoteric and the way of alchemy. It splashes the Dew of the Rose over all earth, bringing the wonder of God's love for man.

"The meaning of the Golden Dawn, Pensatia, is the lifting of the veil of Isis to disclose the Greater Mysteries.

"Now and into the maturity of the Aquarian Age all will gravitate to the White Magic of this Mecca of the disciples of the Rose and Lotus. There on the esoteric mountain top man will bathe in the grandeur of the many-splendoured Flame of Gold. He will know the real meaning is at onement with God and the Masters."

So ends this first chapter of "The Golden Dawn."

❀ Chapter Two

"COME, Pensatia, let us go deeper into the meaning of the Golden Dawn," spoke Master H.

"The Golden Dawn is not an ambiguous figure of speech. It is a living reality, and may be experienced either negatively or positively. Negatively, it is the tool of the left-hand path; positively, it gives man the open sesame to cosmic consciousness. Its divine purpose is to make man aware of his divinity that he may work and serve God and the Hierarchical Brotherhood. Yet man must earn his entrance and this awakening into the Golden Dawn. Only through initiation and braving the esoteric crucibles can the Golden Dawn and the bloom of the Rose and Lotus come forth within one's heart. This attainment is the Mecca of every true student of the Rosy Cross and other authentic Mystery Schools. The Golden Dawn is that cosmic aftermath and fulfillment of man's journey to inner illumination. It is the birth of peace profound after the travail of the Way.

"Without the saving grace of the Golden Dawn man would slip back into the Dark Ages. The cause of all the chaos of world conditions is man's lack of awareness of, and immersion in, the Golden Dawn. This is the atomic secret of the Word. Until man discovers and uses this power for his liberation and to bless and serve mankind, wars and destruction will exist. Only through soul evolution and a breathing in and out of the Golden Flame of this Cosmic Dawn shall man walk again with his Creator and the Hierarchical Masters.

"Like a flash of lightning, man, when ready, can be lifted into cosmic consciousness and the full effulgence of the Golden Dawn, after which life takes on a new meaning, and is seen in a higher dimension of consciousness. The purity and essence of the oneness of the all sings like a bluebird of happiness from one's heart. It is truly a transcendent yet earthly joy when one realizes the Golden Dawn. Its meaning touches everything on earth and quickens one's inner chakras.

"When initiated in this Flame life's vicissitudes and man's self-made karma is liquidated with joy. Even though all earthly possessions may be taken away — riches, love, friends, health — one in faith serves in the Golden Flame knowing this apparent dead-end is only a challenge. It will pass. All one has lost will be returned three-fold. All that is base must be transmuted into the gold of the Elixir and the Stone.

"So with patience, students of the Rose of Life, work in the open sesame of this esoteric Flame. When once in this fire of heaven recede not from it; to do so lifts one back into the darkness of maya's duality and illusions.

"All great paintings, writings, inventions are spawned consciously or otherwise in the Golden Dawn. The whole meaning of this immortal privilege given to man typifies God's love and grace. Man has only to seek and he will find regeneration and illumination. Not the spurious splendor of the left-hand path but the steadfast, redeeming light of the Rose of Life, that immaculate Dew of the Golden Fountain which spirals through man and out to the world. As man bathes daily in its potent radiance he is slowly transformed into his spiritual manhood.

"The meaning of the Golden Dawn is learned by degrees as one faces the dark night of the soul, spoken of in mystic lore. Then suddenly the veil is rent and man walks into the harvest of the illustrious initiation of the Golden Dawn. Henceforth he reflects the glory of the Flame of the Rose. He uses the staff of the Masters. The Word becomes his power. He knows: As above, so below. All the majesty of God's love, mercy and wisdom are showered upon him. The disciple has weathered the challenge of the cross and elevated his consciousness to soul mastery; he is one with God, the Master, nature and humanity.

"Yes, Pensatia," H continued, "the disciple truly has made the esoteric journey into the light. He has won the Golden Dawn.

"I would impress upon all students: Seek not to force the awakening of the Golden Dawn. Rather seek to purify thy body temple, to live naturally, to walk in the crucibles ever lifting your faith to God and the Masters. Keep an open mind toward all religions, getting ever to the core of oneness at their center. See that all obligations are met and your human relations are peaceful and harmonious. Be temperate and keep thy humor clean and bright. Bear all climate of experiences, greeting them as friends and teachers.

"When once you have chosen and placed your feet upon the Path, turn not away even if all else is taken from you. Know when the Golden Dawn touches you the keys to the kingdom will be yours. Such is the meaning and purpose of this secret of the ages, the way to life everlasting.

"When earth doctors become aware of the Golden Dawn true healing will come. Now all areas of science, medicine

191

and surgery are in the throes of experimentation and evolution. Not until those in high places seek and realize the Golden Dawn can they contact and bring forth the cosmic discoveries, the atomic splendor. The coming medicine of the New Age — herbology, color, music — all the cosmic ingredients will be loosened for humanity when doctors and scientists walk and work in the Golden Dawn. All methods used today will pass. In the bloom of the Aquarian Age man will rely only on God, the Masters, and his own self-mastery. He will know nature and the stars, and the sacred responsibility of life and service. He will be at home in the above and the below. He will be able to commune with the sea, the meadowed splendor of wild flowers, the silence of night's tenderness and the voice of the winds in the forests of earth. Truly, in the Golden Dawn man will be attuned with the music of the spheres. The eternal fire of his heart will flow love out to all life and races. The Garden of Eden will open again. All will be at home at last within their Edenic consciousness.

"Yes, the Golden Dawn is the coming forth of the illuminated entrance into the many dimensions and planes of the above and the below. When entering its sacred transcendent light, fulfillment is on all points of the Triangle. In clear consciousness man reads the Akashic Records, he stands on the Most High Mountain of wisdom. Every cell, gland and organ of man takes on the nectar of the regenerating Elixir, one's circulation flows with the cosmic currents. Every department of living reveals its inner signature.

"Here only the tried and tested who are ready for that intimate rapport with the Masters, only those dedicated students who in obedience have persevered through the dark night of the soul, earn the open door of the Golden Dawn. Yet all are free to make the choice, the way is open to all, the Creator plays no favorites. A sincere seeking will open the gate to this afflatus of Cosmic Light. The Rose or Lotus Path, Taoism, Buddhism, Zen, the Way of Krishna, or the Old Rugged Cross will reveal the secret keys to the kingdom. In each is the esoteric door if man searches.

"The Golden Dawn is that center of light which prevails in the wheel of earth life's journey. Many spokes lead to the center; man may choose which spoke to take.

"The spurious left-hand path of the Black Masters never reaches the center. Those who follow this path beguile and use the Golden Dawn for self-power and the riches of earth. By such are wars spawned and crime and sex worship brought forth. All who follow the left-hand path and use the nature spirits for evil are self-destroyed sooner or later.

"Those true to the real Path are protected, naught can prevail when one is nested to the Christ within. The false Golden Dawn exploits its stench in time. The disciples of the Rose Dew learn to discriminate and to ever walk the way to the Most High Mountain.

"So you on the Path and those searching, be ever on guard against the tempters — the professionals of the Black Art. Be not conned into their false allurement and mockery of the real. Ever it is true, when placing one's self on the esoteric journey opposition ever seeks to pull one back. Be steady, strong. Bow not to such pressure and propaganda of the spurious. Let the full meaning, nobility, and Cosmic reality of the Golden Dawn find birth in your heart. Thus can you pass in splendor all the dark nights of the soul.

"Let no negation of thought or action create such karma. Liberate all past incarnations of wrong living and thus prepare for ever greater incarnations of service and love. Start the journey esoteric and you will have the courage to face up to its challenges.

"Such is humanity's goal, spoken in the Word of the Creator; such is the mandate of the Aquarian Age, man-made in the image of God; this, one must be conscious of. Each must learn to walk in the Golden Dawn — this is the fiat of the Aquarian Age. Thus only can wars cease and nature and humanity commune in harmony.

"As one reflects the Golden Dawn so also does he in degree raise the consciousness of animals and those who pass his way. Even plant life takes on a new luster. Even so the climate shows reverence for the working of the Golden Dawn.

"Down through the ages man has pondered and read of the Golden Dawn. To most it is only a fable, a myth lost in the annals of antiquity. Yet its luster has ever existed in all its tangible reality. It glows with everlasting light for man to discover in his own consciousness. Its meaning is austere yet impregnated with the wisdom from the archives of Akasha. It is the luminous beam which lights the way back to the Father's House. To bathe and walk in its golden rays gives birth to spiritual union with God and oneness with all creation, infinite and mundane. It impregnates all the cells, glands and organs of the body; it regenerates one's whole being. It is God's love-breath flowing through the psychic centers of man, awakening him to his divine heritage. It is the cradle of Cosmic birth for man, the secret of Light, Life and Love. To know the Golden Dawn is to bring forth the Rose eternal. Strong, steady and most brilliant its magnificence. Like the splendor of the sun it warms and electrifies one's consciousness with the cosmos, with nature and the brotherhood of man. It is the personification of all man has been seeking down through the ages. No words can describe or do justice to it. Only personal awareness of its dynamic flame can reveal its potent power and wisdom. It liberates and cleans away all residue of grossness in man. Its vibrational flow lifts one's consciousness to the highest realms of spirituality. One may cross safely the Bridge of Vision and partake of all strata of dimension.

"But enough, Pensatia. Let man search the way of attainment. Let him earn the entrance to the inner man, to the golden temple of the heart and the communion with God and the Hierarchical Masters."

✿ Chapter Three

"Now, Pensatia, we will resume with your questions and my answers to them," spoke Master H.

Thus I ask and the Master replies.

Question: Is the Golden Dawn a myth or is it actual?

Answer: It is the true link with man's divinity. Only as man attains such does he have access to the Fountain of Life.

Question: Will the Golden Dawn come to all in the 20th Century?

Answer: It behooves all humanity to seek the Path and prepare for the Golden Dawn.

Question: Can and will man now living survive in the Aquarian Age?

Answer: Only those quickened now can survive into the full Aquarian Age. Once stabilized in the Golden Dawn, man has the protective aura of the Masters and the golden ray from the Temple of the Sun.

Question: Does the Golden Dawn solve all lack of supply?

Answer: All lack of supply comes from negative karma or a want of faith in the Source. Keep faith even when your pockets are empty, gold will come.

Question: Does not the false Golden Dawn give one power and earth riches and all the secrets of nature?

Answer: This may be; but know the spiritual essence is lacking. One has power, but it is inverted for self and the use of the Black Art. All that is false has no foundation or sanction from the Creator, thus the end result is destruction and death.

Question: Is not the Golden Dawn a state of consciousness?

Answer: Yes, it is the awareness of all planes of life, mundane and infinite. It liquidates gross karma into the luminous light of the soul. The longer one stays in its golden altitude and the more one's body becomes regenerated with the Rose Elixir, the greater the attunement with the Masters and the Lord.

Question: Why do so few attain the Golden Dawn?

Answer: Man himself chooses his course. Once set, according to obedience to the Path does one progress. Only at the ripe moment does Cosmic awakening come and man enters the Golden Dawn. To some it happens early on the Path, to others it is a long journey, for many it will not be in this incarnation. Past cause and effect strengthens or weakens man's climb into the Golden Dawn.

"Does the meaning sink in, O reader of "The Golden Dawn?" Are all my words for naught? Is it clear that the Golden Dawn is only your divine Self liberated from the chains of maya and your karmic cause and effect? It is that Light within you, it is the Living Word of the Logos, the awakening of the Rose of Life.

"Let man enter the Path and persevere through all the crucibles, and rest assured there will come that inevitable moment when the glory of that everlasting Flame will be his. Enter not into the Golden Dawn unless directed by the

196

Guru, else the Light blind one. Slow and steady walk the Rose and Lotus Path. Be humble and of good faith, ever listening and meditating in the Cathedral of the Soul. Transmute all into the pure gold of the Alchemist's Stone. Thus in evening hush of day or break of dawn or in reverie all the wonder of the Golden Dawn will sweep over one, bringing soul illumination.

"Yes, the Golden Dawn is the *summum bonum* of man's quest for the Holy Grail. It is the White Magic of biblical days. Its meaning is never revealed in full until one attains. Slowly one works and seeks to open the sacred chakras. When such happens at the right moment and they burst out into that swirling radiance of vibration, henceforth one serves the Masters and humanity according to one's Cosmic mission. One is not aware of this until one quaffs from the divine essence of the Golden Dawn. In comparison all else is stale, drab, gray and harsh. Earth's duality seems reality, maya's illusions joy.

"As one journeys along the esoteric Path one senses with each obedient step a faint glow from the Golden Dawn. One knows if faithful the true harvest will be his. If one fulfills the Cosmic formula, one's realization will bloom into the full meaning and attainment of the Golden Dawn.

"One knows that every effort victorious is impregnated by the Golden Dawn, even though it may be years or another incarnation before the inner awareness comes. Yet it may also come early on the Path. It depends on the student's past credentials or the earning of grace. The first can be last and the last first. Yet ever to walk in its Golden luster is the Mecca of every true disciple of the Lotus wisdom. Without attaining the effulgence of this Light man will never experience the esoteric wisdom of the ages and have dominion over maya.

197

"Remember, this is the law of the Path: As above so below, as below so above. Even as the Golden Dawn glows bright upon the Most High Mountain so must it shine upon the Earth and through man's centers. This radiation from the Temple of the Sun is the saving grace of man. When once anchored in the Golden Flame, no earthly pollutions can penetrate its pristine purity. To stay in it, working, sleeping, loving, means the slow, steady regeneration of mankind. To live outside the pale, not knowing the afflatus of light, is to exist in the darkness of maya's duality, and creates negative karma. The very essence of man's divinity is stifled by man himself. Only by conscious realization will one attain the Illustrious Dawn."

Now the Master paused. Turning, his eyes penetrated the very depth of my consciousness.

"Pensatia, the time is ripe for the Wisdom Path to open wide for man to enter if he will. The decision is his. God and the Masters never force. The Masters point the way, for they have journeyed and won the citadel of the Rose within the heart's temple high in the ramparts of the sun. They have braved the crucibles of the Alchemist, made gold, and hence give gold. The Elixir they have found. Thus may all who walk the way of the ancient Rosae Crucis.

"Hard and rugged the Path? Yes, yet ever blessed by the love flame of the Golden Dawn. Nested therein lies the secret of life. Only in this golden bath back of the earthly sun is the regenerating power of the Word, and love such as no mortal knows who has not been lifted into the dynamic flow of this infinite light.

"Much repetition is given you, Pensatia, that over and over the potent laws be impregnated in the reader's mind. Remember, my messages are not given as masterpieces of language or polished words to please the elite and intelligentsia. Neither are they written to be best sellers. No *real* artist or writer ever uses his brush or pen to please the public. Rather he is dedicated to create as his soul and heart inspires. To do otherwise is to put commercial and world fame first, thus destroying one's Cosmic mission to create. To prostitute writing or art for a passing flash of pleasing the masses, the effort soon dies, even as cults. Only that spawned from the soul lives eternally. To make one's habitat in the Golden Dawn brings green harvest. The law of recompense ever sees that just dues come to the dedicated artist and writer. It may be long or short in coming, but come it will. So be content with herbs and bread, give thanks for humble fare, never doubt that the banquet will come. Never lose your faith. Go to the Source for all things. Turn on the light within and all will be.

"Only in the center of the heart will one find all wisdom. Nothing outer, no person, can give man the Rose of Life, save himself. No exoteric wealth can buy man the Golden Flame or create the Philosopher's Stone. Naught but walking the Path, working in the crucibles, a pure dedicated heart and obedience can bring attainment. Have these credentials and one will find the Secret of the Ages, that Dawn beyond the earthly sun."

❀ Chapter Four

Now the Master bore me upward into that vast silence of spiritual dimension, there where in golden splendor were gathered the Hierarchical Conclave bathed in the aura of celestial heights. A pulsating awareness was mine. It was as if God spoke through the golden hush, saying,

"Such is the mandate of the Word, the mandamus of the Creator. It is man's destiny to achieve the glory and peace of the Golden Dawn."

The Golden Dawn is a meaningless myth unless realized by man. Then one sees into the Alpha and Omega of life. He knows oneness with God's creation; he knows the love of brotherhood. Science and art open up and reveal their mysteries. Out of the Golden Dawn come the sages, the philosophers, the adepts, the initiates and disciples; these are the wayshowers of the Path. From the Light the secret of life everlasting is revealed.

Now indeed the splendor of Light silhouetted from Cosmic mountain top and poured with the Rose Dew over and through us and down to the dark planet Earth. We heard the AUM sound forth, heard the trumpet of Archangels, heard the joyful song of birds, and all was peace and harmony. We saw a healthy humanity clad in beautiful flowing robes, saw merry children playing in meadowed daisy fields, saw great green-limbed trees shading silver running streams. Clean and fresh the air. Such will be the glory of the Aquarian Age, made so by the Golden Dawn — that immortal Flame which quickens all earth and humanity into oneness with the Creator.

It was awe-inspiring to witness the panorama of the New Age. One felt the impact of the Living Word, felt love radiating through all and everything, felt the peace of the evening hour, heard the music of the spheres mingling with the soft winds of earth. Saw we the beasts of the wild tamed by the spirit of man, saw the rivers and air of earth pure again, saw cities clear of slums, saw brotherhood walking the land in one accord, saw simple values prevail, saw nature, herbs and cosmic knife taking the place of drugs; music and color lifted man to cosmic healing. Saw we man and woman mated through divine alchemy, saw love again a many-splendored reality.

As we gazed in Akasha's heights we saw the karmic cause and effect of past civilizations, saw the printing in Akasha over-shadowing cosmic war, saw the redeeming Golden Dawn — the liberator of man — blazing luminously, calling nations to embark upon the mystic Path and thus save Earth from annihilation. Saw we the Hierarchal Masters, they of the White Brotherhood, ever working, serving to lift man into the Golden Dawn. Saw we the purging of earth, the weeding out of negative hate, greed and slaughter, saw we communion and mastery of the higher dimensions. Heard we music transcendental pouring through man. Saw we masterpieces of art representing heavenly scenery, and art of the Golden Dawn, visual, vital, and of brilliant color.

"Yes, Pensatia," spoke the Master, "you are witnessing the New Age of Aquarius to come. Those who enter within the heart and find the key to the Golden Dawn will surely see the breathing of love upon the land. They will partake of the green harvest. Yes, the Garden of Eden men shall discover within themselves. The Kingdom of Heaven shall flower and all men will worship in the Cathedral of the Soul. Thus will the Creator's Will be done on Earth as in Heaven. The Rose Dew will refreshen and water the land. Resurrected will be man's cross. The stone from the sepulchre will be rolled away. The Living Christ will be born in the heart of man. Soul will be the Master. All will live in their Body of Light. All will live in dignity and honor."

The Akasha screen faded from view. We, the Master and I, bore down to earth dimensions. How dull and heavy seemed the polluted air and turmoil of earth's chaotic strife.

How dark the groan of war, the cry of man enslaved by self-made chains of maya.

The Master spoke.

"Heed not this man-made travail. Center thyself in the Golden Dawn, the glory of God's mandate, and know the world will surely come into that promised land of light, life and love. Ever see above, beyond the darkness. Have faith. Journey to the Most High Mountain. Doubt not, for the Aquarian Age shall bloom, the beasts of the wild be tamed, the apex of the pyramid be built by man. Laughter clean and fresh, love true will mate man and woman. All life will reflect the Creator. 'Well done,' will resound from the Heavenly Host, 'Satan is redeemed, the Black Art lives no more. The Golden Dawn comes forth.' "

My heart sang. I knew the Master spoke true, knew the spiral is ever upward, knew peace would come.

"Yes," echoed H, "peace will be. The true Light of the East will be given by those who have experienced the Golden Dawn. Yes, when the pupil is ready those who know and are guardians of esoteric wisdom will surely give to the student that he may also experience first-hand the light within. No wisdom is ever given to him who stands in the East unless he knows the Light. Wisdom is not entrusted into the hands of those who know not the Living Rose, for the time comes when they have nothing to give. Alas, too many leaders are spurious and know not the heritage of the sages. All they give is empty words, the truth they cannot impart for they have it not themselves. Thus decay, intellectualism and materialism destroys that which should be dedicated to the awakening of the Golden Dawn.

"According to the illumination of esoteric leaders so will the Hierarchal Masters bequeath to them the wisdom from the Cosmic archives. Such illumined leaders, yet humble and dedicated, surely are the chosen ones esoterically. To them is entrusted the wisdom of the Greater Mysteries. Such are beacons of the Golden Dawn. They exemplify the Living Rose and draw many to the Path. Ever they carry out their Cosmic role under the guidance of the Hierarchal Masters. To be in their presence is uplifting, one senses their alchemical prestige. One feels the inner authority of their Cosmic role. Such is the nobility of a real leader of the Living Rose and Lotus. Such is the power of those who have experienced the Golden Dawn. They give out because they have. The music of the spheres ever sings through their hearts. The Golden Dawn flows through them a dynamic light out to life, drawing mankind to the portal of the Path. Without the knighting of the Golden Dawn all knowledge is only of the intellect, as cold and lifeless as dead ashes — no warmth of heart, no radiance of wonder, joy and love to give, just outer emptiness.

"All cosmic consciousness is spawned in the Golden Dawn. Without the illustrious Golden Flame the inner chakras could not bloom and man would be fated to the slavery of maya and its duality. Yet the Creator of all life willed otherwise. In His beneficence and love He brought forth the Golden Dawn of the Rose and Lotus. Brought He forth the Elixir and Stone. Brought He forth the Avatars — those venerable wayshowers who lighten the ignorance and lift the consciousness of humanity to a higher level. Brought He forth the Living Word and the White Lotus of eastern lore. The laws of the Cosmic were etched in Akasha for man to learn. The kingdom of heaven was placed in man's heart, in the temple of the Golden Dawn. Gave He man chance after chance through the laws of reincarnation. Revealed He through the Christus the crucifixion and resurrection of the cross. Through nature's seasons was taught the inner meanings of life. All aspects of nature were given to man to master.

"So you see," spoke the Master H, "the Golden Dawn is the luminous trail to the heaven within. It is the Path of the Christus, Krishna and the Elect.

"In the days of Atlantis the Golden Dawn was the search. Then, the Sons of the Solitude using its golden power for materialism and selfish use, destroyed great Atlantis.

"This golden spray from the Oversoul contains the key to all strata of consciousness. Without its Cosmic Illumination man could never find his way back home to the Father's House. In the parable of the Prodigal Son the fatted calf is the Golden Dawn personified. After partaking of the husks of life man returns to the riches of the gold of the Flame of Life.

"I hope the reader of these talks, given through Pensatia, will awaken a zest to enter the Path and find for himself the Golden Dawn. May all feel the call of the Path of the Sun Temple high in infinite dimensions, there where the Rose Dew regenerates and the Lotus of the heart blooms in all its celestial power.

"The Golden Dawn is that magnetic pole of balance making possible for man to know his God. It is the arrow of peace making active and productive man's soul consciousness. It is the tidal wave of cosmic consciousness sweeping man into his divine destiny."

204

❀ Chapter Five

"How does one attain this cherished plateau of consciousness? To aspire is not to attain. To read of its function, its illustrious credentials, will not lift you to bathe in its Cosmic Light. No drugs, LSD or mushrooms will open the doors; these will give you only the false and cannot sustain you in the Golden Dawn. There is only one key which opens the door to this Dawn: A sincere dedicated heart, utter surrender to the Creator and a deep desire to know the Masters.

"One must choose an authentic outer portal, an Order sponsored by the White Lodge. After choosing, one must go through boot training and eliminate all negative karma, transmute all lesser attributes into the gold of the alchemist. One must through obedience and patience, through love, joy and inner awakening of soul power cross the bridge to the Most High Mountain. This is not easy. There is no short cut to the Golden Dawn. It is a steady, sure, often slow expansion, not an artificial mockery of the real. To breathe its immortal flame one must have faith which no mundane opposition can shatter. There must be absolute experience with Cosmic and natural law. One must acquire all in positive action, thought and service to God, nature and man. A divine steadfastness must ever be to attain discipleship and make true this aged saying: 'When the student is ready the Master appears.' Would you reach this Cosmic Golden Dawn? Patience and obedience and working with infinite law will surely lift you into the shining Dawn of life everlasting. One must pass the Ring of Saturn, be initiated in earth, water, air and fire. One must lose all to find all. One must walk with nature and learn from its innermost heart. One must partake of the song and dance of life and bring forth laughter and joy. One must meditate, pray and love greatly. One's consciousness must be at home in Akasha, must be free from the astral. One must dare all strata of dimensions in infinite altitude. One must master each step before going to another. One must ever worship in the Cathedral of the Soul and be baptized in the Dew of the Rose. One must ever hear the music of the spheres through all life, and love earth as much as heaven. One must clear and transmute the earthly body from the gross and negative so that the Body of Light be the director over all one's actions. One must acquire that divine inner wisdom and strength which does not crumble from the stress of changing maya and outer stress of opposition. Yet one must ever be pliable, mutable, and ever attuned and obedient to infinite law.

"Yes, Pensatia, pen clearly this inevitable mandate: The Golden Dawn is a reality and will in the full Aquarian Age be the conscious awareness of every true disciple of the esoteric Path. Without this grace man is empty and barren, he has lost contact with his divinity. To live in the Golden Dawn is life, health, wealth, and a walking with God and the Masters. It is conscious oneness with the whole wide world, and a knowing — not a believing — of the wonder of cosmic consciousness and those mighty men of present and past sagas. The Golden Dawn is the illumined benediction of a Creator's love for His creation. It is the shining Grail awakened in every heart, the celestial music of the spheres flowing through man himself. To attain this golden attribute of the Godhead man must empty himself of every material objective and the negation and duality of maya. And as Samuel of old he must say, 'Here I am, Lord, use me as Thou wilt.' One must brave the alchemy of the Rose and transmute all the dross in man to the pure gold of the soul. One must sweep away the cobwebs of the past and swim towards the horizon of the Aquarian Age we are now entering. One must liquidate all into Cosmic light. Heaven and earth must mix and the twain become one.

"The Golden Flame consumes those not prepared. Those negative shysters of occult lore still are seeking to use this power for personal gain and to use their evil magic to enslave others. But the Cosmic law is: 'He who seeks the Golden Flame for aught but the Living Rose shall surely perish in the Flame.' Yet, again and again the Black Masters seek to overcome infallible laws and destroy the White Magic of the Golden Dawn, held by the White Lodge in escrow until man earns the right to enter its luminous brilliance. One passes through many stages, sometimes several incarnations, before he attains the golden shower of man's dawn of inner light. Then again it may be attained in the present life if one applies one's self in dedicated obedience to the Path. With application, service, love, courage and faith man will surely attain. The Golden Dawn flows on through nature and man, ever waiting to enfold humanity."

Now the Master H did take my hand and led me into the swirling vibrational splendor of the Golden Dawn, yet all seemed peaceful and a clear vision was ours. The whole world, the planets, the very secrets of nature were accessible. It was truly fourth-dimensional sight, hearing and feeling. Every thing on earth and in heaven was seen in its spiritual essence.

Spoke H: "The goal of man's purpose is to know the inner signature of all life. To know only the material, objective side of earth is to lack the perfect balance and harmony of living. In the attainment of the Golden Dawn one realizes at last the full meaning of his divine heritage. The Golden Dawn is the awakening of that Light within. In it is all and everything of transcendent and earthly wisdom.

207

To bathe in it daily engenders health, youth and the call to one's mission. As the blood is to the earthly body so is the Golden Dawn the circulation blood of the Cosmic. Without this consciousness man is little more than a robot or zombie. He walks the earth not realizing the light within. Only by seeking and finding the Path of the Golden Dawn will man obtain immortality. As one seeks, so will he find. Ask, and the way will open to you.

"There is a Golden Dawn even as there are the Masters, even as there is the 'Lost Horizon.' Students of the red Rose and of the Lotus, you who tread the upward trail to illumination, persevere. Back not down into the bogs of maya, rather follow the call of the Golden Dawn. Let not your steps falter until you bear witness to the shining gold within your heart. There is no experience in life comparable.

"Again one asks: What is the meaning of the Golden Dawn? how does one attain it? and how does one know? These three questions are really bound in one answer, which is: A consciousness, an awareness, a new Cosmic perception, a new birth into one's Body of Light, a wondrous glow, an inner peace which transcends all harshness of life's storms and chaos of ever-changing maya. The bitter and sweet become understandable. One sees fourth-dimensionally. Cause and effect are made plain.

"Like a cleansing baptism the Golden Dawn erases and clears body, mind and heart of all dross and negation. One is attuned with the music of the spheres and feels compassion for those still enslaved in ignorance. One feels the needs and sorrows of the world, not in spurious sentimentality but in constructive understanding and aid. Such is the magnitude and healing light of the Golden Dawn. It liberates and brings forth the divine afflatus within man. It is the Cosmic touch of man's awakening into the center of his being, the consciousness of the Holy Grail, the birth of the Christ within the heart of man."

Thus closes the fifth chapter of "The Golden Dawn."

The Master departed, saying, "We meet again at the opening of the sixth chapter."

❀ Chapter Six

"The Golden Dawn is not a barren fulfillment of the Path but bears a rich harvest of all degrees. One's first contact with its transcendent soil lifts man into the endless bounty and realization of the alchemist's dream — the Stone and the Elixir. One knows at last his labor on the esoteric Path of Rose and Cross is not in vain. All his toil, obedience, his experiments, his initiations bear witness to one's entrance into the Golden Dawn and the clear light of Akasha granted him. Now henceforth he walks, works in communion with the Masters and Cosmic altitude. Having weathered the climb so far upward, now he must merge the lesser into the higher and the higher into the lower. He must learn to gauge the earthly under the laws of the Golden Dawn. The love fluid must be poured through all earth avenues. He is aware that all things of earth have their divine counterpart. All is known in its divine signature. A new dimension of the consciousness has been awakened, henceforth he lives from an added frontier. All earth life is seen and felt under the light of the Golden Dawn, he marvels even as he learns to walk and work in it. At first its high voltage of altitude is breathtaking. Unless well grounded in one's boot training foundation the activated inner senses can be overwhelming. Little by little one must embrace and learn the mode of application. To be explicit, one must learn to live in the light of a new dimension yet not lose the value of old frontiers of living. There must be a cosmic fusion, a harmonious mating of the two — the ecstasy of earth must feel the ecstasy of cosmic afflatus. Remember, in the lesser is found the higher, and in the higher the lesser. The attainment of such comes through walking and mastering one step at a time on the Path. Like a seed planted in earth loam man cultivates the seed of the Golden Dawn within himself until by one's own efforts, in maturity of consciousness, the Golden Dawn arises in splendor in the heart of the pilgrim to the Most High Mountain. It is indeed a most gratifying journey — the self-discovery into one's being, the toil within the alchemist's shop. Nothing can compare with the reward of turning 'base metals' into 'gold.' No joy so great as the flooding of the Golden Dawn upon man. He knows at last the meaning and realization of the kingdom within . . . he knows God *is*. He has pierced the veil into Akasha, and walked the Bridge of Vision. He has witnessed the oneness of all life, heard the song of the spheres, he has braved the initiations of earth, water, air and fire and emerged victorious. Such is man's reward as he walks into the cosmic ramparts of the Golden Dawn. All the soft whiteness of the Christ spirit glows through the earth life of the student. Sweet splendor seen from man's inner sight reveals beauty and purity in all creation.

"Is it not worth it, Pensatia, to endure the discipline of the Way, the alchemical crucibles, the obedience of the Path of the Rose that one may attain the truth of the Golden Dawn and be liberated into one's divine self? The White Magic of the lost Atlantis comes to birth in man through the Golden Dawn. One realizes how barren and empty was one's life before the chains of maya were freed from the objective self. All the glory of a new stratum of consciousness blossoms from one's centers or chakras. No longer is man adrift on the Sea of Maya, he is catapulted into the Mecca of his cosmic consciousness. He has proven to himself the immortality of consciousness. From then on he lives, works and serves in the Golden Dawn. Balanced on all points of the Triangle, one sees the chaos of world affairs, senses the turning away from God's infinite pattern; all the maze and duality of maya is felt. Yet also in the Golden Dawn is revealed the working and infallible harvest and spiritual renaissance breaking like a tidal wave into the Aquarian Age, washing away the dross, the spurious and false and making life into the likeness of man's divine legacy.

"Yes, man will break through this decadence and emerge into cosmic adultship. Soul wisdom, soul power, soul light will flood man's consciousness. He will know the inner workings of mind, body and soul. He will not be satisfied with only temporal knowledge but will seek the Path leading to the Golden Dawn. The self-made veil of ignorance will be lifted. Those who cling to the old status quo will surely perish in their own ignorance, for the Aquarian mandate is: Man, know thyself.

"All pioneering efforts into the inner depths of man are rugged. Yet as man perseveres and seeks the Golden Dawn he will know that brilliance of a new tomorrow. All will be synthesized into the whole of earthly and heavenly splendor; the two will weave and merge as one.

"The White Magic will be victorious over the Black. Atomic power will bless mankind. The true values of the old dispensation will be held sacred while embracing the new wisdom of Aquarius. Every man will hear the call to the God within and to the flow of the Aquarian Water-pitcher. Those who recede will banish themselves from the light of the Golden Dawn. All that is false or contrary to the wisdom of the ages will fall away. Naught but justice, balance, equality and brotherhood will prevail. Nature in all its beauty — trees, plants, animals — will be reverenced and preserved.

"Those who are the forerunners, those who have traveled the road upward to the Temple of the Sun, those hardy, faithful pioneers will surely reap the harvest and the 'well done' of the Masters. They will know where others merely theorize or have only intellectual knowledge of such.

"Such is the Master's message recorded by Pensatia that you might sense the road ahead to the Golden Dawn, and in a small measure glean the great journey man must make in some incarnation. The Golden Dawn, labeled by many names, is the jewel of great price spoken of by the Essene, Jesus, the Christed One, and all the sages of all ages. To attain it one must follow closely the Path, taking nothing with him save his naked self free from all sham. As a child one must seek to earn the grace of the Golden Dawn. One must ever rise into cosmic consciousness and experience the transmutation of one's lesser self. As one obeys and faces the crucibles of alchemy, little by little man's inner chakras light up and revolve upward until at the ripe moment they are centered into the Golden Dawn. Henceforth man walks, works, loves and serves in the new vibrational splendor of the Golden Flame. Therein is found the lost Eden, Shangri-la, the heaven within, and all the joy of earth life also. The labor of achievement is forgotten in the joy of the birth of the Golden Dawn."

So ends the sixth chapter.

❁ Chapter Seven

"PENSATIA," spoke H, "the Golden Dawn is the natural budding into bloom of man's seeding in one's journey into the Light. It is that communion with Cosmic dimensions and that silence within which is golden. It is the music of the spheres singing the song of creation. It is the outpouring of God's love lifting man to his infinite destiny. It is the calm and peace of nature in the hush of evening when the stars look down and bless all mankind. It is the fresh twang of sea winds calling to man to love and live and search for the Golden Dawn. It is the AUM, the eternal sound of heaven, drifting earthward into the hearts of men. It is the alchemical gold of the Stone and the Elixir. It is the transcendent flame of Isis unveiled, the miracle and wonder of life.

"All and everything is the Golden Dawn. The healing waters of life, the joy and wisdom of nature bloom out to man their ageless panorama of inner secrets. The most arduous toil becomes a spontaneous work of poetry. Sorrow and joy are muted messengers of Light. One carries on his earth life in stability and cosmic order. In all earthly relations, like the melody of a nightingale, man walks, works with purpose and dignity. Man feels alive for the first time, yet he realizes he has earned this clearness of vision. He has step by step attained mastery over his lesser self; he knows there is no short cut to the Shangri-la of soul consciousness. He has borne witness to the rising of the kundalini. Water, earth, air and fire have baptized him. He has lain on the Field of Ardath and heard the voice of the Lotus.

"Yes, the Golden Dawn is the synthesis of the whole coming to life in man. It is the breakthrough of the waters of life bathing man into the awareness of cosmic consciousness. To attain this fulfillment the esoteric student must

213

diligently obey the boot training. Step by step he earns the way to the mountain top of the Golden Dawn as he walks and works in the crucibles of transmutation. The agony and travail of the masses seeking escapism mock and ever seek to crucify one's journey to the Golden Dawn. Yet the faithful disciple of the Rose and Lotus walks on, ever becoming inwardly stronger and drinking of the wisdom of the gods. He performs his tasks with joy, he keeps merry and daily attunes with nature. Right where he is the disciple applies all he has learned from the reservoir within.

"As you sprinkle the Dew of the Rose on all actions and deeds you are ever drawing closer to the awakening of the Golden Dawn. The attributes of the Body of Light grow and mature as man cultivates its acquaintance. There comes a time when one is objectively and inwardly conscious of his spiritual body. When this happens you have arrived, so to speak, at the very heart of the Golden Dawn and the impact of your spiritual birth. In this epochal birth man knows he is a living soul in a temporal body. He realizes his soul now is master and director of his life. No longer does one cater to the dictates of his earthly vehicle. One is the slave no longer. His soul is the captain and in obeying one ever walks and works in the Golden Dawn for God, the Masters and humanity. To attain this afflatus of the Holy Ghost one must pass through the crucifixion and Gethsemane of the cross. One must experience the rolling away of the stone of the sepulchre and the resurrection of the Christus in man. The birth of the Christ babe takes place in the Temple of the Sun, the place of the thousand-petalled lotus located on top of the head. There, when initiated, the floodgates of the Golden Dawn liberate man from the duality of maya and make all things new; one is indeed born into the heaven within.

"As the novice dwells upon the meaning of the Golden Dawn he begins to realize the dignity, the dedication demanded of the neophyte. However, the journey, the curriculum may seem too severe for the weaklings, those who seek an easier route to the Golden Dawn. Alas, there is none! They find this out to their sorrow. Thus in leaving the one sure Path to the Golden Dawn one leaves it for the spurious 'fool's gold.' One becomes a mystic tramp, seeking but mastering nothing. And finally one becomes a doubter, a disillusioned, weak and sorrowful derelict, or else sells his soul to the Black Masters. Readers, find the true Path and earn your way to the mountain top and the Golden Dawn of the Living Rose.

"The Golden Dawn is the awakening of the Holy Ghost, the power of the Word flowing through man as his inner chakras open to the floodlight of cosmic consciousness. It may come at any moment when the person is ripe. It may come slowly or burst forth like the sun. But come it will to the faithful disciple. He will then know the Masters are, God is, and the oneness of all life. He will be content to walk the earth in the supreme light of his soul. Naught of objective happening can mar the peace profound that realization of the Golden Dawn gives one.

"Thus we see the Golden Dawn is the Mecca of all true esoteric students. From the very beginning of their earnest steps along the Path they feel the promise and fulfillment of the Golden Dawn. With each victorious step and victory in boot training an inner stability is achieved, a living faith in the search of the alchemical Rose and Elixir. An inner surety that the crucibles are not in vain stirs faith in one's heart to ever strive for the awakening of the Golden Dawn in the temple of the Lotus. To attain the very first inkling of this inner splendor one must want it more than breath.

215

One must earn from bedrock! To assimilate all its ingredients one must harmonize with its interior message. One must ever, with humble allegiance to the Rosy Path, hear the song of the Creator. One must discard all non-essentials and cleave only to the boot training of the journey to the Golden Dawn. Stillness of body and mind is essential, and unwavering obedience to the God within. There must be that all-out surrender to the tutelage of the Master within. One must be willing to face past karmic debts and omissions and transmute them to the aura of the Golden Dawn. One must turn a new page and be willing to be born anew. Thus only will one walk and live in the Golden Dawn."

Now the radiance of the Golden Dawn spiraled over and through us. A relaxing stillness like hushed music prevailed in the atmosphere. Our whole being was lifted into Cosmic Consciousness. In golden light which billowed into snowy whiteness, our thoughts, our vision, our senses leaped into life beyond the objective. We were indeed immersed into the heart of all dimensions. The hum of the AUM was ourselves, and we the AUM. Such peace, joy and happiness was never felt by mortal ken.

"Behold, Pensatia," spoke H, "we are standing in the flame of the Golden Dawn. All our senses radiate, see and hear in the fourth dimension. No longer are we bound by the objective duality of maya. We are able to see all in its Cosmic signature. We stand four-square in the limitless splendor of the Golden Dawn. Such is the reward of the pilgrim of the Rose and Lotus. Such is the awakening of our chakras into the infinite wisdom of the soul."

The Golden Dawn was part and parcel of our being. A synthesis of all life flowed in vibrational splendor through body and mind. Our hearts were open to the thousand-petalled lotus. The stone of the sepulchre was rolled away.

In liberation from maya's shackles we knew and walked in the Light. Earth became a reflection of the above, and the above existed below.

"Pensatia," said the Master, "the Golden Dawn regenerates man into the fulfillment and meaning of soul consciousness. Man is able to travel in all dimensions earthly and heavenly. He has indeed crossed the Bridge of Vision. He has reached the citadel of the Most High Mountain. No longer does he enslave himself in ignorance and destructive karma. He has become reborn into the Golden Dawn."

❀ Chapter Eight

I NOW resume my contact with the Master H. His voice speaks through the silence of the heart.

"Pensatia, many will question this book of the Golden Dawn. Its mythical background and esoteric lore is likened to the fabled Elixir and Stone. 'All is abstract and there is no earthly foundation,' the ignorant layman will say. 'It has no reality in the objective world of practical living.'

"Alas, that this is so. Nevertheless, in spite of the masses' rejection of Cosmic truth, esoteric books have lived through the ages and proclaimed the Golden Dawn, its meaning and attainment, to the few initiated ones, to the disciple of the Rose, to the sincere seekers of the kingdom of heaven within. They who hunger for the awakening of the Golden Dawn, they who treasure all light that flows from the pen. Thus those channels of esoteric contact ever serve humanity through pen knowing there are always those selective ones who catch the message and start the journey to the Golden Dawn. Such will have Cosmic blessing and, if worthy, will, when ready, come under the tutelage of the Masters. Not the spurious charlatans, those Black Masters of deceit and dark powers, but the true Masters of the White Brotherhood and Hierarchical Conclave. Such are the august members of the true Golden Dawn and the immortal Rose of Life. Such were Hartman, Boehme, Blake — all initiates. Such were all the Avatars of history. They sought only the alchemy of the soul and thus found all else. They sought the gold of heart and mind, sought the stillness and peace within where no outer storm can destroy. In doing so the Master came and led them to the Most High Mountain and the Golden Dawn.

"Yes, readers of this recorded journey by Pensatia, my amanuensis, there is a Golden Dawn, stable and uplifting, scintillating with the love ray of life everlasting. It alone carries the secret of the ages, the great healing force, the power to master space, the power to unify and bring peace to all the land.

"Without the Golden Flame man is benighted as though in the dark ages. In the influx of the Aquarian Waterpitcher the Golden Dawn will prevail. Man no longer will live in negation and ignorance of his dignity. No longer will religion be a man made orthodoxy but all will worship in the Cathedral of the Soul. In the temple within all will commune with nature green and wood-bound stream. Merry laughter will resound. Wisdom will be sought. The Golden Dawn will reign, love and peace make happy the earth.

"This is God's fiat for man: Consciousness and life in the Golden Dawn. In the New Age war and strife will not prevail but will go down in their own self-making cause and effect. Fall will all chicanery, all that bears not the stamp of the Aquarian signature. The AUM of the music of the spheres shall be heard by man. Purified, the air. Gone, the weapons of atomic design. All energy will be harnessed and

218

used for humanity's benefit. The values of the old will be revived and wedded to the wisdom of the Golden Dawn.

"In toil and labor the student builds the foundation. He adjusts to and breathes the altitude of a new dimension. He becomes one with Cosmic Law. Akasha's print becomes readable. He learns the ingredients of the Stone and Elixir. In the crucibles he becomes the alchemist, making gold and giving gold. He awakens to the privilege of life and pays homage to God and nature. All this is attained by obedience to the esoteric Path one enters.

"No longer is he a follower of the five senses, in seeking and attaining the Golden Dawn he awakens the inner chakras. In doing so he has access to all the gifts of the spirit. But this does not come about by mere wishing. First, one must prepare body, heart and mind to receive the coming of the Golden Dawn. One must transform all negation and wrong habits into harmony with their God-self. Every step upward must be earned. All mandamuses in the outer school must be assimilated and put to use in life. One must prove first-hand all experiments given, otherwise his knowledge is only intellectual. Only from personal awareness can one know the Golden Dawn. No mere reading of external study will lift man into the arena of the Golden Dawn. No dilly-dallying on the outskirts, one must brave the initiations of earth, water, fire and air. One must go through 'Dante's Hell' and come forth in Heaven.

"One must choose an outer school and adhere through all exterior opposition. One must with patience toil in the crucibles to transmute all into the pure gold of the soul. One must master the fundamentals of earth and synthesize all into the celestial whole. To attain this precious heritage of man one must surrender everything of earth on the altar of service and cry out: 'Here I am, Lord. Use me.' As one obeys, so hastens one's awakening into the Cosmic afflatus. One cannot attain this august achievement with money, or by spurious methods, or the joining of cults. Only that open heart and faith of a child will unlock the door to the Golden Flame. Only dedicated prayer and obedience to that fabled Path within, to that sacred place of peace profound within the human heart. Attainment of the Golden Dawn is of paramount importance in this, the Aquarian cycle. It is the Savior of mankind. One who has attained this Light will lead the world to the citadel of the Aquarian Waterpitcher, the Golden Dawn which has existed down through the ages.

"Yes, a leader will come forth who will lead humanity into green pastures and beside still waters. He will exemplify the Golden Dawn and reveal the way to peace and fulfillment of man's esoteric destiny. Those who heed will seek and find the way to the Golden Dawn.

"Life's melody — the upsweep of Aquarian waters — is purifying and washing away the dross of man's stain. The karmic mistakes of all races must be liquidated, else in atomic flame the world perishes.

"So man, listen to the Cosmic harmonium. Listen to the song of the bluebird. Know thyself. Commune with sea, woods and mountains. Realize the interchange of thought."

So closes the eighth chapter of the book of "The Golden Dawn."

❀ Chapter Nine

"THE GOLDEN DAWN is not as austere or arduous to attain as the preceding chapters would seem to indicate. Only to those who try to skip the boot training, or desire quick results, or those who seek to utilize the inner Path for personal gain — only to these is the Path dangerous and seemingly worthless. It is good that the weak ones soon eliminate themselves. They then claim that the Path is false and has no worth. Such ignorant ones of their own free will walk out, becoming lost in their untruths. Often, not for another or several incarnations will they be able to contact the Path. For in Akasha it is written: One who heeds not the opportunity of Allah, or the Creator, will forfeit such at another time; opportunity will pass him by.

"There is a flood tide which calls man to action. The wise man heeds and thus changes his life for the better. Remember, and remember well, no call comes to one who is not ready; no door opens that one cannot enter. Those who tarry on the outskirts are existing only on the husks.

"The Path of the Golden Dawn will belch forth those who dare betray or use for self alone its ancient laws. To partake of the essence of the Golden Elixir one must surrender his all to the God of all people. One must mix the earthly elements into the heavenly altitudes and weave them into the wholeness of the Golden Dawn. When one sees the Light in every thing and in every person, when one hears the song of life surging through nature and man, when one has known sorrow, loss, pain and ecstasy and is content and happy to let go of all earthly props; when one can smile in the midst of tears, when one travels upward no matter how rugged the way — know that one has attained or will attain the Golden Dawn. It is a matter of obedience, application and patience. The formula for attaining is the love flame of the heart flowing ever outward to life. It is the act of renewing the self from within and drinking from the water of life everlasting. It is the breathing in the rhythm of the Oversoul and being aware of the pulse beat of the Creator. It is being natural, simple, ever walking in the profound heart of nature. It is communing in that golden thread which unites all races into that oneness of love universal.

"To attain this exalted consciousness one must leave all and tread the Path upward with faith, obedience and joy; one must liquidate all past negative cause and effect and build anew. Thus will the Golden Dawn be yours into the Land of the Leal. Thus will you be at home in all climes. Thus will you walk in the high mountains of the soul, and even into hell your Light shall shine. The way of the Path you will exemplify for others. The song of life will surge through you out to the dark night of the world. You henceforth act and serve under the Cosmic flag of the Golden Dawn and 'Well done' will be said of you. The travail of your soul birth will be forgotten in the glory of the Golden Dawn."

Now the Master H pondered a moment, then spoke in quiet dignity yet with strong cadence:

"Behold, Pensatia, within man shines that Light not known in land or sea, shine the sacred chakras waiting to be awakened into their spiral to the God Jehovah, Gitchimanitow the Mighty. At the base of the spine, coiled, lies the kundalini, which when raised to action makes man master of himself. Yes, imprisoned by the ignorance of man shines the Golden Dawn.

"Now in this atomic age, in this Aquarian cycle, the clarion call comes forth: Awake, you who sleep. Hear the bells of Kismet pealing out the summons to seek within the Path to the Golden Dawn. Hear the singing winds, the tramp of the beasts of the wild, the surging tides of high seas. Hear the groan of nature as it senses man's degradation and betrayal of his God-self. List again to the God within. List to law and order, the Golden Rule. List to the Cathedral of the Soul, to meditation in the hush of eventide. List to the way of the Rose, to the lesson of the Lotus. Let your chakras open slowly, as the planted seed in earth flowers into blossom. Listen and heed the voice of the Master within in stillness and meditation, in prayer. Dedicate thy efforts in obedience to the Path esoteric. There abide until you are victorious through all strata of consciousness leading to the Golden Dawn.

"The way of attainment is long, stern are the requirements, yet great and lasting the results. The Golden Dawn is man's credentials to the kingdom within. To attain it means conscious access to all the dimensions of earth and heaven. One may scan the alpha and omega of creation and know first-hand. Here and in the hereafter one is at home in all climes. Man worships in the Cathedral of the Soul and the chimes of infinite melody uplift and inspire him. He sees the aura of nature, man and beast. The ninth vibration of love flows through his blood and heart ever out to all earth and humanity. Such is the power of the attainment of the true Golden Dawn, of the Rose and Lotus, of Tao, Kaballa, the way of Zen, the Bhagavad Gita, and the Essene Jesus, the Christed One. Such is God's gift to man when he earns it.

"Like a melodious lullaby, the slumber of him who attains is peaceful and regenerating. At daybreak his awakening is refreshing, his adoration to God and the Rose of Life, everlasting. His work in the world, menial or otherwise, takes on a new dimension of service. A living faith is his. He stands a man foursquare, his vision of immortal value, yet sired in the loam of earth. With a humble, joyous heart he walks out into life bathed in the Golden Dawn. Strong, vital, a true representative of the Rosy Cross, or the Aquarian Waterpitcher.

"Such is the mantle of the Golden Dawn. As one's consciousness is lifted into its transcendent Light one knows, where before he doubted the spiritual verities. Yes, to enter the Path esoteric and attain this altitude of awareness is the sum total of God's love for His creation.

"To the masses the Golden Dawn is usually an unheard of fiction. They spurn its existence as they do fairy tales. To them it is a far-out myth. The few who seek and question are bent to explore the truth for themselves, they search within and dare. Thus the Masters draw them to the Path of the esoteric way after testing their sincerity and courage. As neophyte postulants they start their pilgrimage to the Most High Mountain and Golden Dawn. The Hierarchical Hosts rejoice for well they know: He who starts, obeys and walks the mystic Path will find liberation from the chains of maya. All who find the illustrious Flame of Gold will in greater or lesser degree become lights on this dark planet, Earth, for as they receive they bear out to life its magnetic rays. Such spring up to live again no matter how demagnetized they were. The dynamic Golden Dawn heals, blesses, prospers all who abide in its Cosmic rays.

"So, readers, if you would have health abundant, love and life, enter the esoteric Path. Let the Rose bloom from the Cross of Matter. Let the Aquarian call of the Masters be heard. Know, dare and do.

"The Golden Dawn awaits man's entrance into its sublime radiance of action and green harvest. Steady, sure and expansive, it is the true essence of life's secret back of the sun. It is the sum total of God's gift to man. It is the Father's love, the Masters — those White Brethren — spilling the wonder and fulfillment to man, earthly and heavenly.

"All the dynamic magnetism of life flows through the Golden Dawn down from Cosmic heights, through man and out to others. Man must attain it to survive in the Aquarian

Age. It is simple, profound, natural. Only from within himself can man enter its healing flame and be born anew.

"All the Hierarchal Masters serve to draw humanity into their divine Shangri-la within. You earthlings, build your foundation. Enter the door to the light of the Golden Dawn. See beyond the objective into the Cosmic whole. Find that magnetic coil which lifts man to awareness of mastership. What matter the slow, hard steps? From the first sincere start your faith and obedience will see you through until, when you are ready, the beloved Master makes known his presence and leads you out of the darkness into that luminous Light generated from the orb of the Creator's love. Therein the singing music of the spheres will harmonize all the base notes in your physical nature, and faith justified will reveal: Not in vain the long pilgrimage to the Golden Dawn.

"Little by little as you start the esoteric Path of Kaballa, Rose or Lotus you will find the veil of earthly mist and ignorance lifting until one day you walk at will all dimensions of thought and action. Your life and deeds will reflect the glow of the Golden Dawn within you. No longer will it be a myth but a reality you have with you always. This will not come about in spurts and artificial 'mumbo-jumbo' but through slow, steadfast adherence to the boot training of the mystic Rose, Kaballa or Lotus. It will not come by mere study of the written mandamus but by dedicated application and work in the labyrinth within. It will not come about by wishful reading or jumping from one door to another. Only by obedience to the Path and Cosmic laws will one realize the Golden Dawn. It is man's right when he earns it. There are no special privileges, all must take the King's Highway to the High Mountain. All must attain by way of the cross. All must seek and create the fabled Stone and Elixir, and make gold and give gold. They themselves, must mine the gold; no 'fool's gold' can buy one the key to the Golden Dawn."

The Master turned and journeyed up to the Mountain of Light.

"Pensatia," echoed his words, "rest in earth's climate. We will meet at the tenth chapter."

"So be it," I answered, and lowered my consciousness to earth's loam.

❋ Chapter Ten

"THE GOLDEN DAWN, its meaning and attainment, are woven together like Siamese twins. Both are one. To realize the meaning is to realize the attainment. The meaning possesses the open sesame to Shangri-la. It liberates the singing winds of heaven through man's awakened chakras which hence flow out to earth. Like the steady drop of rain nurturing the seeded loam, thus bringing forth luscious fruits and blossoms, making green the land, so the steady application of the mandamus of the Rosae Crucis brings forth the Golden Dawn — that Light of which spoke all the Avatars, and lastly the Essene, Jesus, the Christed One. That Light found not on land or sea but in man himself.

"When the Golden Dawn bursts forth like the glowing sun man is truly baptized in the waters of life everlasting. No longer do the tides of mundane life affect him. No longer do the stars dictate to him. He has mastered his astrological pattern and attained his esoteric chart. Only then do the Masters know the golden signature of the student. Yes, not until the student has proved himself and relatively mastered his mundane karma do the Masters take him under their wing, so to speak, and henceforth guide the potential disciple within and up to the Golden Dawn of Cosmic-oriented man.

"The Masters are ever faithful to their Cosmic mission, ever aiding the disciple in all ways feasible by rule of the Lords of Karma. Yet the student decides by his actions and obedience the opening of his chakras and his entrance into the immortal Flame of Isis. Like a seedling in the ground the student cultivates the nucleus of the Light within himself by obedience to the mandamus of the Rose and ever transmuting the gross elements into the pure gold of the Alchemist. All progress comes in relative degree until in one burst of awareness the Dawn illuminates all life. The inner signature of earth in all its ramifications becomes an open book. He is one with earth and heaven. He senses the inner heart of God's manifestation. He revels in the colors and glory of creation. He knows humanity is moving ever upward to the holy mount of the Golden Dawn. He hears the singing bells of endless dimensions. He has experienced the depth and ecstasy of life. He has transcended death into life everlasting. Regardless of the ever-changing faces of maya, he knows within the calm of the heart center that the profound peace of the Rose in bloom is his. So let the wild winds blow and the beasts of earth growl, let ignorance seek to destroy, let the rumble of war and lost values walk the earth — he who has attained the Golden Dawn knows this, too, shall pass and man shall triumph as he enters the Aquarian Age.

"So hasten, people of all nations, seek and enter the Path to the Golden Dawn. It is now, and ever shall be, man's soul freedom from all the duality and ever-changing maya. It is the eternal sound, sight and Light ever flowing from the Word down to man when he opens the channel within himself. It is the wisdom of the Oversoul speaking through man, the magnetic caress of God's love, and the Master's call to discipleship.

"To seek and find the Golden Dawn is to be aware in consciousness of the oneness of the universe and to be able to travel at will through the endless dimensions of creation — not for earthly gain, or physical power, or occult control of man and nature, but only for love and service to God, the Masters and humanity.

"The Golden Dawn bequeaths to man that attainment of clear perspective, it lifts man into the secret archives of the alpha and omega of life. Its magnificent splendor covers man like a golden robe. Like a gentle earth mother, it quickens and brings forth the divine in man. In its beneficent Light one's whole being has rapport with both earth and heaven. It is as if the blood and soul of man are of one twain, as if through the alchemical marriage love's bounty, earthly and heavenly, is given to man. The divine is wedded to earth, and earth to heaven. Henceforth the Golden Dawn sings through the heart of man the glory and meaning of his Creator.

"The Golden Dawn is the pulsating flow of Cosmic attainment, that radiance of soul consciousness bestowing wisdom and usage of God's eternal purpose for man. It is the fulfillment and mastery of man's divine destiny, the full bloom of the afflatus of dimensions of awareness. Man arises in the Golden Dawn, speaks, acts and moves ever in obedience to the God within.

"Until one attains the altitude of Flame one is empty, barren of true soul awakening. So it behooves man to ever explore this lost horizon of consciousness and enter the esoteric pilgrimage to the Most High Mountain. Step by step as man walks the way of the Path he liberates the mortal man into the immortal until on attaining the Golden Dawn he knows he is a living soul in an earthly body. Having full awareness of his Body of Light it henceforth is the master, not the slave, of his physical vehicle. He is indeed knighted by the Holy Grail and the love and blessings of his Heavenly Father. He has won the pearl of great price, and love's splendor crowns him. He realizes life is eternal, consciousness is forever. The many mansions are his to choose from. Liberated from maya's duality he works ever from the finished kingdom. His aura shines with the love caress of the Golden Dawn. The music of the spheres flows its melody through him and ever out to humanity.

"Yes, all humanity at some time in its many incarnations must and will attain the Golden Dawn and know God is, and the Masters are. Even as Jules Verne foretold in fiction the many scientific discoveries of today, even so down through the ages the Rosae Crucis and the ancient archives spoke of man's conquest over ignorance and the Cosmic Illumination of his entrance into the Golden Dawn.

"Yes, people of earth, your heritage is divine mastery over the lesser. Stand up tall in the sun. Through the loam of earth seek the Path to the Golden Dawn within yourself."

❀ Chapter Eleven

AGAIN spoke Master H from the vast reservoir of Cosmic Hierarchy.

"Pensatia, our talks concerning the heart and soul of the Golden Dawn are drawing to a close. May all who read my words glimpse in some degree its meaning and attainment, and may those not yet in the outer temple receive the urge to seek and know this grace of the Creator and knock at the outer portal, and thus start the pilgrimage to the Golden Dawn.

"I know of no attainment which brings fulfillment to one in every aspect of life as does the Golden Dawn. It carries one through the Gethsemane of earth travail and clarifies all meanings not understood. It is God's gracious 'Well done' given to man when he earns it. It sweeps one's consciousness into the sublime oneness of creation and humanity.

"Without this attainment man flounders in hopeless confusion and emptiness of mind and heart. One may try all the devious routes of escape with drugs, alcohol, LSD, etc., only to find there is no shortcut to soul wisdom or escape from one's divine self.

"The Cosmic mandate is: Go forward into the Lotus Wisdom or perish in the negation of one's own cause and effect.

"Only a turnabout, a true seeking of the Golden Dawn and its attainment will bring forth that peace profound from out the heart of man. Humanity can evade it no longer and continue to survive. All must reflect the heart of the Creator. All must know the truth that God *is* and the Masters *are*.

"Archeology is daily revealing truths long hidden. The depths of the ocean are unveiling what the sages have known in ages past. The time is at hand when Cosmic law takes command over earth laws and all that is not in harmony with man's spirit must and will vanish from the earth.

"The Golden Dawn, its meaning and attainment, reveals the saga of man's journey to the esoteric mountain top of inner wisdom. It is the start of guidance to the homeland of the Shepherd of life, light and love. In this Aquarian Age man must ever seek to know and find the open door of attainment. The glorious rainbow in the heavens proclaims

God's promise that if man searches he will find. In time all men's chakras will open and receive the Golden Dawn pouring forth in its spiraled activity fresh from the High Mountain. How wondrous this gift of God's love! When man experiences such he is indeed forever blessed, he lives in the finished kingdom deep in that hidden temple of his heart.

"That immaculate flame forever glowing in the esoteric center of the heart is ever there for man to discover. No matter what happens to the human heart nothing can kill that Cosmic spark of the Secret of the Ages — the Golden Dawn, that breakthrough of the Sun of Life back of the earth sun. It is the vestal fire which stays with man until the silver cord is broken and then flies with man to heavenly mansions. It is man's comforter through all the sorrows and crucibles of one's earth journey. It is the mirth and bubbler of life, the gentle love of man and woman, the refreshing inspiration of Cosmic splendor, the revelation of wisdom, and the melody of earth and heavenly music. It quickens fortitude, courage, and gives man insight to all dimensions.

"Yes, readers, the Golden Dawn is the saviour of mankind. It liberates one into the Christus of the Holy Grail, the esoteric Kaballa of Moses, the truth of Taoism. In it one is attuned to all the Avatars, Sages, Masters, past and present. People of all races become united in friendship and scintillate to the flow of the Aquarian Waterpitcher. No longer is one enslaved by the illusions and duality of maya. One rises in a glorious oneness with all life. Man has found that peace profound, that ultimate reality of soul consciousness.

"This is no fantastic dream but a practical print of God's mandate for humanity. Slow, steady application and refining man's outer grossness, complete dedication to the Path, walking close with nature, laughing and loving much, forgiving and compassionate with all, brings one to the flame of attainment.

"Oftentimes the more one advances on the esoteric Path the less he is understood, even by his loved ones. He is accused of being self-centered and selfish. Often, as his aura increases and his vibrations become high people either love or resent him. In these tests bear with patience and forgiveness and love those who know not what they do. In time even those who stone you will gravitate to you and bless you. Yes, this too will pass. Walk on, fulfill your mission. Be fluid and adaptable to all experiences. Keep your soul integrity even in 'Dante's Hell.' Thus will you ever stand erect in the Golden Dawn and come forth the illumined Rose of Life."

❁ Chapter Twelve

"Now the curtain falls on this, the book of the Golden Dawn. Like the delicate scent of temple incense or the attar of roses, may the indelible truth of the meaning and attainment of this Golden Dawn in some measure stimulate your inner search of such. May it clarify the real from the false. May it call you to walk the Path of the Lotus and the Rose. May this climactic awakening be yours so that the gracious peace and wisdom of the Masters bless you, and your days be long, and the mirth and joy of the yellow robe of Isis Unveiled be given you.

"Now let me reveal one more attribute of the Dawn. Its golden splendor is ever sired and matured in its basic foundation and stability of silver.* This ingredient must be real-

---

* See "The Master H" by Pensatia, page 110.

ized by all students of the Way. Until one acquires and is aware of the silver balancing the Golden Flame one may never attain the golden luster itself. Thus, to be brief, one must be initiated into, and utilize all the basic ingredients of the Golden Dawn. One must not seek the Flame until one has the silver foundation and inner stability, that inner fortitude, to walk in the Golden Flame. Without the awareness of the silver one is stranded in the Flame, unprepared to handle it.

"Silver is demanded in all the attainments of the esoteric Path. So you who would attain the Golden Dawn, seek first the balancing fusion of silver; thus will your growth be sure and steady. Remember this, all you who are neophytes or disciples-to-be.

"The silver ingredient will make one strong, steady, and able to partake of the Golden Dawn in safety and Cosmic fulfillment. So many students forget this, thinking only of the Golden Flame. They do not take the basic steps or realize the formula they seek. They seek only to attain, evading the Cosmic mandate of 'first things, first.' Thus they fail and are lost in the brilliance of the Golden Dawn. They are not stabilized enough to stay in it, thus exiled by their own cause and effect. They denounce the Way and henceforth become mental hoboes, reading, attending and hearing lectures, but mastering nothing.

"All must acquire silver to attain. Remember, earth and heaven both are fused in the shining gold of the Dawn. One is useless without the other. 'As above, below; as below, above.' So read the records of Akasha.

"I speak of the silver lastly because I want you to realize the importance of silver in your esoteric journey. It is the most valuable of all ingredients. To obtain it makes it impossible for one to slip back into the prisonhouse of maya, and makes certain the ascent to the Most High Mountain. I speak lastly of it for the disciple must discover this truth himself and realize it. The Master will reveal it when the student is ready. After the silver is awakened and working in and through his centers he will know, the Golden Dawn will break through to him. Gold cannot be appreciated in its Cosmic value unless silver be appreciated first. Let this Cosmic law sink into your heart, and ponder.

"May the reading of this book clarify the ledger and truth of the Golden Dawn. And may you in time through work and service find the Living Rose which ever shines through the Golden Flame.

"Yes, there is the Golden Dawn, most tangible and real. Its fabled history veils the truth until man himself discovers it. He who walks in the Golden Dawn has found the Secret of the Ages. This is the goal, subconsciously, of all man's journey through 'Dante's Hell' to the illumined initiation on the Most High Mountain. As the sun shines after the night, so man rises in consciousness of the Golden Dawn and walks in the Light to ever greater service to God and humanity.

"So mote it be for all who find and tread the Way."

. . .

. .

.

This volume was designed
and printed at the office of the
Peter Pauper Press
Mount Vernon, New York